MATH DETECTIVE®
B1

S0-BDT-469

Higher-Order Thinking·Reading·Writing in Mathematics

SERIES TITLES
Math Detective® Beginning
Math Detective® A1
Math Detective® B1
Reading Detective® Beginning
Reading Detective® A1
Reading Detective® B1
Reading Detective® Rx
Science Detective® Beginning
Science Detective® A1

Terri Husted

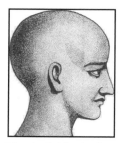

© 2005
THE CRITICAL THINKING CO.™
(BRIGHT MINDS™)
Phone: 800-458-4849 Fax: 831-393-3277
www.CriticalThinking.com
P.O. Box 1610 • Seaside • CA 93955-1610
ISBN 978-0-89455-864-1

Printed in the United States of America

To my husband Dave
and my children Alexis and Venissa.
Thanks to my editors Maggie Hockett and Cheryl Block.

TABLE OF CONTENTS

What is Math Detective®?

Introduction

The problems in this book will improve your students' skills in mathematics, critical thinking, reading, and writing. The topics and skills covered are drawn from the national standards for mathematics for Grades 7–8, as outlined by the National Council of Teachers of Mathematics. The problems are short, easy to use, and fun for students.

Problem solutions involve critical thinking and careful reading of text, charts, graphs, and tables. Students are required to explain their thinking in writing.

Students are frequently asked to support their answers with evidence. The evidence cannot be uncovered by scanning the text, but instead requires in-depth analysis of the information in the text, diagram, or both. Information in the text may include irrelevant information or scattered information, necessitating careful reading and analysis. This analysis develops good reading comprehension and critical thinking skills.

The questions in Math Detective® are modeled after questions found on new math assessments, but require more extensive critical thinking. These problems are excellent preparation for assessments that require students to explain and support their answers.

Also included are a chart of key ideas and topics, as well as all answers and solutions.

When to Use The Math Detective®

Math Detective® can be used to help introduce or review topics in your math curriculum. Math Detective® is an ideal solution for test preparation because it does not teach to a particular assessment. It develops the skills needed to excel on new assessments. In field-testing with students in Grades 7-8, Math Detective® was highly effective in clarifying topics that students had found confusing in previous years. It is also a wonderful source of enrichment activities.

Grades 7–8 Math Standards

The math topics covered in this book are organized around the strands outlined by the National Council of Teachers of Mathematics: Number and Numeration, Operations, Geometry and Spatial Sense, Probability, Statistics, and Algebraic Concepts. For a detailed list of all topics covered within each of the key ideas, please see the Table of Contents (page iii) or the Key Ideas and Math Topics chart (page vii).

Many problems contain important math vocabulary. Some of these terms are defined in the problem, and some must be identified through context clues in the story.

Reading in Mathematics

Many math students have trouble reading in general and do not understand the importance of reading in mathematics. Math Detective® teaches students to read carefully by requiring the students to identify evidence that supports their answers. In fact, students must often identify information from multiple sources (text, diagrams, and other graphics) and synthesize these different pieces of information to arrive at the answer. The depth of analysis needed to solve these problems develops thinking skills and improves reading comprehension.

Written Explanations

Many questions in this book ask students to use complete sentences to explain their thinking. The ability to express their thoughts—supported by evidence—in writing is not only important in math assessments, it is essential when communicating with other people in school and work. It also promotes better understanding of the mathematics being studied.

Despite the growing trend to evaluate written explanations and support of solutions, many math students score poorly on these test items. The carefully designed questions in Math Detective® will develop thinking, reading, and writing skills while they prepare your students for new state math assessments.

If a student has trouble writing about how she solved a problem, ask her to explain her solution aloud then guide her on how to write the explanation. Remember, it helps to model your own thinking on how you solved the problem, and then ask the student to model her own thinking. Showing work in a neat and organized fashion is also stressed. A separate introduction and sample problem with solutions has been provided for the student.

Thinking Cap Questions

Some problems are questions that go beyond the literal and, at times, interpretive levels of thinking. Such problems are designated by a detective cap, as shown.

KEY IDEAS and MATH TOPICS

NUMBER AND NUMERATION (Lessons 1–7)

Topic	1 The Summit Summer Camp	2 The Prime Dart Game	3 Let's Have Some Order!	4 David's Division Dilemma	5 The Amazing Mayans	6 The Planet Report	7 The Percent Building
Bases					X		
Commutative Property			X				
Division Concepts			X	X			
Exponents					X	X	
Fractions (%)							X
Least Common Denominator	X						
Multiples	X						
Percent Concepts							X
Place Value					X		
Powers of Ten						X	
Prime Numbers		X					
Reading Numbers						X	
Scientific Notation						X	
Whole Numbers (+ or -)		X					
SYNTHESIS (Combines information from multiple sources to draw conclusions.)	X	X	X	X	X		X
OTHER MATH TOPICS							
Logical Reasoning	X						
Multicultural					X		
Reading a Chart	X						
Trial & Error		X					
Vocabulary				X			

OPERATIONS (Lessons 8–13)

Topic	8 The Roberts Family Reunion	9 Classroom Supplies	10 Getting Ready For Track	11 The School Election	12 Don't Spill The Black Beans!	13 The Taxi Investigation
Decimals (+ or -)						X
Decimals (x or ÷)		X	X			X
Equation Concepts	X					
Fractions (+ or -)			X			
Fractions (x or ÷)				X	X	X
Least Common Denominator		X				
Percent Concepts		X				
Rounding	X		X			
Reducing Fractions				X		
Whole Numbers (+ or -)	X			X		
Whole Numbers (x or ÷)						
SYNTHESIS (Combines information from multiple sources to draw conclusions.)	X	X	X	X	X	X
OTHER MATH TOPICS						
Measurement			X			X
Money Sense		X			X	
Multicultural	X					
Reading a Chart						

RATIO, PROPORTION, AND PERCENT (Lessons 14–19)

Topic	14 Making Maple Syrup	15 Testing Time	16 The 8th Grade Dance	17 Eddie's Cat Rescue Gone Wrong	18 The Furniture Store	19 The Better Deal?
Decimals (+ or -)		X			X	
Decimals (x or ÷)			X	X	X	X
Decimals (%)					X	
Equation Concepts			X			
Fractions (x or ÷)				X		
Fractions (%)			X			X
Percent Concepts		X				X
Ratio and Proportion	X		X	X		
Similarity			X	X		
Solving Proportions	X	X				
Whole Numbers (+ or -)						X
Whole Numbers (x or ÷)			X	X		
SYNTHESIS (Combines information from multiple sources to draw conclusions.)	X	X	X	X	X	X
OTHER MATH TOPICS						
Interest						X
Measurement	X			X		X
Money Sense			X			
Multicultural	X					
Reading and Making a Chart			X			X

KEY IDEAS and MATH TOPICS

Activity legend (column numbers):

20	The Three Triangles
21	The Area Competition
22	The Geometry Quilt
23	The Rectangle Resort
24	The Octopus Intersection
25	Soccer Abroad
26	The Tale of the Math Garden
27	Designing a Slide
28	The Potato Delight Store
29	The Display Dilemma
30	The Custom License Plate
31	The Big Jolly Jelly Beans
32	Winning the Shopping Spree
33	Battle of the Video Games
34	Great Books to Read
35	Dream-On Survey
36	Farming Our Town
37	The Mean Rainfall
38	Circle of Pizza
39	Expression Session
40	The Bacteria Investigation
41	Quane's Quarter Collection
42	Barrow, Alaska
43	The Calendar Magician
44	Differing Degrees

GEOMETRY

Topic
Angles
Area
Inequalities
Parallelogram
Perimeter/Circumference
Rectangles
Square Roots
Symmetry
Triangles
Trigonometry
Volume

PROBABILITY

Topic
Combinations
Counting Principle
Factorials
Permutations
Decimal (+ or x)
Finding Odds
Fractions
Money Sense
Multi-stage Events
Two-stage Events
Whole numbers (- or x)

STATISTICS

Topic
Bar Graphs
Circle Graphs
Function/Multiple Representation
Intro to Algebraic Expressions
Line Graphs
Mean, Median, Mode and Range
Pictographs
Proportions
Ratio
Reading and Making a Chart
Conversions
Decimals (+ or -)
Decimals (x or ÷)
Fractions (+ or -)
Fractions (%)
Fraction Reducing
Logical Reasoning
Measurement
Money Sense
Percent Concepts
Vocabulary
Whole Numbers (+ or -)

ALGEBRAIC CONCEPTS

Topic
Algebraic Expressions
Associative Property
Commutative Property
Concept of a Variable
Distributive Property
Exponents
Function/Multiple Representation
Integers (+ or -)
Integers (x or ÷)
Inverse Operations
Order of Operations
Solving Equations
Coordinate Graphing
Decimals (x or ÷)
Intro to Logarithmic Curve
Measurement
Money Sense
Reading and Making a Chart
Whole Numbers (x or ÷)

OTHER MATH TOPICS

Topic
Coordinate Graphing
Decimals (x or ÷)
Logical Reasoning
Measurement
Powers of ten
Pythagorean Theorem
Ratio
Reading a Chart
Reading a Map
Solving Proportions
Vocabulary

SYNTHESIS Combines information from multiple sources to draw conclusions.

SCORING RUBRIC/ASSESSMENT CRITERIA

Each complete Math Detective® activity includes a story and questions related to that story. Questions may require arithmetic computation, identification of evidence, and explanations of the student's thinking. Therefore, to get a good picture of the student's overall performance on an activity, a 3-part scoring rubric is suggested. First, mark individual questions to indicate errors in computation, identification of evidence, and clarity of the explanations. Using a photocopy of the rubric below, combine the informal assessments to generate an overall 3-part score for the activity.

- -

Student Name _____

Activity _____

THREE-CATEGORY SCORING RUBRIC

- Content understanding (student understands concept, recognizes patterns)
- Clarity of student's explanations (complete sentences, clearly written)
- Accurate computation of answers (correct arithmetic computation)

Content: If the information in your answer showed complete understanding of the information in the story and graphics, you got a 3. If it showed a partial understanding, you got a 2 or 1. If there was absolutely no evidence that you understood the information, you got a 0.

Clarity: If you communicated clearly, even if the ideas themselves were wrong, you got a 3. If your ideas were communicated poorly, you got a 1 or 2. If you were not clear and it was impossible to understand your thoughts, you got a 0.

Accuracy: If the computation for all arithmetic problems was correct, you got a 3. If only some of it was correct, you got a 1 or 2. If none of it was correct, you got a 0.

Content Score: _____ (Scale 0–3)

Clarity Score: _____ (Scale 0–3)

Accuracy Score: _____ (Scale 0–3)

Comments:

_____

_____

_____

_____

To the Student

Why You Should Become a Math Detective®

Critical thinking, reading, and writing are as important in mathematics as they are in the rest of your subjects. This workbook was created to improve your thinking, reading, and writing skills while you learn and practice math.

It's All About Evidence

As a critical thinker, you need to look for evidence in what you read. Evidence is information that shows why something is true or could be true. Read the six sentences below and try to find the evidence that tells you who was into the peanut butter and jam.

[1]Eddie's mom looked at Eddie and baby sister Sarah. [2]There were crumbs on the floor, and Sarah had peanut butter and jam on her chin. [3]"Who got into the peanut butter and jam?" asked Eddie's mom. [4]Eddie told his mom that little Sarah had eaten the peanut butter and jam. [5]He quickly grabbed a paper towel and put some water on it so his mother could wipe Sarah's chin. [6]As he handed the towel to his mother, she noticed peanut butter and jam on Eddie's fingers.

Information in sentence 2 tells us that that "Sarah had peanut butter and jam on her chin." We know from this evidence that she was into the peanut butter and jam. Sentence 6 tells us that Eddie had peanut butter and jam on his fingers. We know from this evidence that Eddie was into the peanut butter and jam. The evidence in sentences 2 and 6 shows us that both Eddie and Sarah were into the peanut butter and jam.

The questions in these activities sometimes ask for the sentence(s) that provides the best evidence for an answer. To help you identify a particular sentence, all the sentences in the stories of this workbook are numbered. Some questions may require you to give the numbers of one or two sentences AND find information from a diagram to answer the question. You may have to go back and search the text or story for the sentence or sentences that contain the evidence you need to prove your answer is correct. All critical thinkers reread what they have read to make sure they understood what was written and to be sure they did not miss any information. In this book, YOU ARE THE DETECTIVE; that is why this book is called *Math Detective*®.

Sample Problem

The Camping Trip

[1]The Lee family was going camping. [2]Mr. and Mrs. Lee woke up at 5:30 A.M. and began to load their van with the tents, cooking utensils, and suitcases. [3]Mrs. Lee began to put all the food in the cooler. [4]Mr. Lee woke up his children, Abe and Sakai, at 6:45 A.M. [5]Abe remembered to feed their dog, Bubbles. [6]Abe said, "Come on, Bubbles, eat fast! [7]Everywhere we go, you go!" [8]Sakai chose to stay in bed until the last minute. [9]The family left at 7:15 A.M.

[10]As they left, Sakai said to her mom, "Mom, may I have some coffee? [11]I've been up helping for three hours."

[12]Abe said, "Liar, Liar, pants on fire!"

[13]Mrs. Lee said, "Now Abe, I want no fighting on this trip. [14]And as for you, young lady, you can forget about drinking coffee!"

[15]The total trip took six hours. [16]The family would have gotten there sooner but they took a 35-minute rest stop to have lunch.

Questions

1. How long were Mr. and Mrs. Lee awake before Mr. Lee woke up Abe and Sakai?
   _____

   Give the numbers of the two sentences that provide the best evidence for your answer. _____, _____

   Solution:

   1 hour and 15 minutes

   Sentences 2 and 4

   (We know from sentence 2 Mr. and Mrs. Lee woke up at 5:30 A.M. , and from sentence 4 that Abe and Sakai woke up at 6:45 A.M. The time difference from 5;30 A.M. to 6:45 A.M. is 1 hour and 15 minutes.)

   _____

2. What time did the family arrive at the campsite? _____

   Give the numbers of the two sentences that provide you with the best evidence for your answer. _____, _____

Solution

1:15 P.M.
Sentences 9 and 15.
(We know from sentence 9 that the family left at 7:15 A.M. and from sentence 15 that the total trip took 6 hours. Given the information in sentences 9 and 15, the solution must be 1:15 P.M. because if we add 6 hours to 7:15 A.M., we get 1:15 P.M. Therefore, sentences 9 and 15 provide the best evidence [support] for the answer.)

3. If the family had not stopped, at what time would they have arrived? _____
    Use complete sentences to explain your thinking.

Solution

12:40 P.M.

(We know from question 2 that they arrived at 1:15 P.M. Sentence 16 states that the lunch break took 35 minutes. We can take 1:15 P.M. and subtract a half-hour, which would give us 12:45 P.M., then subtract 5 minutes from 12:45 to get the answer.)

4. Which of the following conclusions is supported in the problem? Circle the letter of the best answer.

    a. Mr. and Mrs. Lee did all the cooking on the camping trip.

    b. Mrs. Lee does not like coffee.

    c. Bubbles, the dog, came on this trip.

    d. The family traveled by way of plane.

    Give the number of the sentence that provides the best evidence for your answer.
    _____

Solution

c.
Sentence 7.
(We do know from sentence 5 that Bubbles is the dog, but in sentence 7, Abe says that everywhere the family goes, Bubbles goes. We don't know for certain that Bubbles did go, but sentence 7 provides the best evidence that Bubbles travels with the family.)

Choice a is not a good choice because we have NO evidence from the reading to know that Mr. and Mrs. Lee did all the cooking on the trip. Just because they packed a cooler doesn't mean they cooked all the food on the trip.

Choice b is not a good choice. Just because Mrs. Lee doesn't let Sakai drink coffee doesn't mean Mrs. Lee herself doesn't like coffee.

Choice d is incorrect because we have no evidence that the Lee family took a plane. We know they were loading up their van.

5. Why did Abe say: "Liar, liar, pants on fire!"? Use complete sentences to explain your thinking.

_____

_____

_____

_____

Solution

Abe said this to his sister because she was in bed until the last minute (sentence 8), so she could not have been up helping for three hours. Also, if she was awakened at 6:45 A.M. (sentence 4) and they left at 7:15 A.M. (sentence 9), then she had not been up three hours!

Math Detective® Certificate

Awarded to

for

Date

Signed

Math Detective® Certificate

Awarded to

_____

for _____

Signed _____

Date _____

I
NUMBER & NUMERATION

1—The Summit Summer Camp

[1]At the Summit Summer Camp, lessons are offered according to children's ages. [2]The Garcias have four children who want to join the camp during the summer. [3]Luisa and Martha, who are twins, are four years younger than their oldest brother Carlos. [4]The twins both want to sign up for swimming and skating lessons. [5]Carlos is the only child in the Garcia family who is eligible to take rock climbing lessons. [6]Luis is eligible to take all three of his favorite sports: soccer, swimming, and skating.

[7]Swimming lessons are offered every two days. [8]Baseball lessons are offered every three days. [9]Skating and rock climbing lessons are offered on the same day every five days. [10]Soccer lessons are offered every four days. [11]The rest of the time, arts and crafts, and free time for swimming in the pond are allowed for all the children. [12]The camp is open for forty days.

Complete the age chart to help you answer the questions.

	AGES
Martha	
Luisa	
Luis	
Carlos	

LESSONS	FOR THESE AGES ONLY (in years)	HOW OFTEN
Swimming	10–14	
Baseball	10–12	
Skating	12–13	
Rock Climbing	14	
Soccer	13–14	

Questions

1. How old is Carlos?

   a. 15   b. 10   c. 13   d. 14

   Give the number of the sentence that provides the best evidence for your answer.
   _____

2. How old are Martha and Luisa?

   a. 11   b. 10   c. 12   d. 13

   Use complete sentences to explain your thinking.

   _____

   _____

3. Are Martha and Luisa able to sign up for both of the lessons they hope to take? Use complete sentences to explain your thinking.

   _____

   _____

4. How old is Luis?

   a. 10   b. 12   c. 13   d. 14

   Give the number of the sentence that provides the best evidence for your answer.
   _____

5. How often does Luis have all his lessons on the same day? Every _____ days. Show your work.

6. How many times during the entire camp session will Luis have his three lessons on the same day? _____ Show your work.

7. How often will Carlos have his lessons on the same day as the twins? Every _____ days. Show your work.

2—The Prime Dart Game

¹Ian and Lisa played a new game of darts that Lisa's grandfather made up when he was a child. ²When Ian saw the dart board, he said, "All the numbers are odd numbers." ³Lisa's grandfather said, "You're right, Ian. ⁴However, all the numbers on the board are also prime.*"

⁵Ian said, "Yes, it has the smallest prime and then a few more."

⁶Lisa's grandfather then said,

"Actually, the number 3 is not the smallest prime, Ian."

⁷To play this game, Ian and Lisa were told to throw four darts. ⁸A player would get 10 points if the sum of the four numbers was 100. ⁹However, if a player got a sum of 43 with three darts, he or she would get 43 points!

¹⁰Ian asked, "Why is 43 so special?" Lisa answered, "Probably because 43 is also a prime!"

* A prime number is any whole number after the number 1 that has only two factors, 1 and itself.

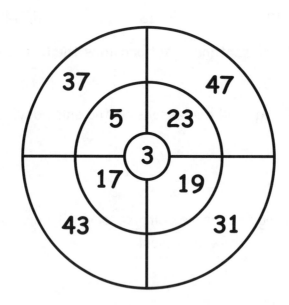

Questions

1. The numbers on the dart board have all of the following properties in common EXCEPT one. Which is NOT true?

   a. Each is divisible by 3 or 5.
   b. Each is an odd number.
   c. Each is divisible by itself and 1.
   d. Each is a prime number.

   Give the number of the sentence that provides the best evidence for your answer. _____

2. Lisa played the game and got 10 points. List at least two different sets of numbers she could have hit.

   _____

   Give the number of the sentence that provides the best evidence for your answer. _____

3. Which is the smallest prime number?

   a. 0
   b. 1
   c. 2
   d. 3

4. Ian got 43 points on his turn. What numbers did he hit? _____

   Give the number of the sentence that provides the best evidence for your answer. _____

5. The numbers 17 and 19 are called "twin primes" because their difference is two. List all the sets of "twin primes" that are less than 100.

3—Let's Have Some Order!

[1]Mr. and Mrs. Ross and their children, James and Amy, are going camping. [2]James is helping his dad pack the van. [3]They have the tents and the cooler and their clothes all ready.

[4]Mr. Ross says to James, "We must make sure the cooler goes into the van first. [5]That way we can reach the food from the back seat if we get hungry during the trip. [6]The clothes should go next. [7]The tents go in the van last because we will need to take them out first when we get to the campground. [8]Once the tents are set up, we can unpack the rest of the van. [9]So, you see James, the order in which we pack the van really matters."

[10]James replies, "Dad, the order in which we do things always matters. [11]After all, putting on your socks before putting on your shoes is different from putting on your shoes and then putting on your socks!" [12]Mr. Ross laughed.

[13]Amy, who is listening, says, "Now, wait a minute. [14]In math, I can show you an example where the order doesn't matter. [15]If you add 5 + 7 you get the same answer as 7 + 5." [16]She adds, "So if I want to eat the cookies from the cooler now instead of waiting until we get to the campground, it should not matter."

[17]Mrs. Ross interrupts, "Oh no! It's going to be a very long trip if you both start arguing and eating too soon! [18]Besides, in math, just like in everyday life, sometimes order matters and then there are times when order doesn't matter. [19]Both of you better come up with some examples in math of what I mean. [20]That will keep you busy in the car until we get there!"

Questions

1. Was there a reason for packing the van in a special way? _____

    Give the numbers of the sentences that provide the best evidence for your answer. _____, _____, _____

2. Which of these examples shows that the order in which you do something sometimes matters?

    a. Taking a shower and drying yourself OR drying yourself and then taking a shower

    b. Adding 6 + 7 OR adding 7 + 6

    c. Multiplying 5 X 8 OR multiplying 8 X 5

    d. Putting your right shoe on and then your left shoe OR putting your left shoe on and then your right shoe.

3. The property that allows you to get the same answer when you change the order in which you do an operation is called the <u>commutative property</u>. Circle the problems for which the commutative property works, and put an X by the problems for which the commutative property does not work.

    a. | 4 + 1   1 + 4 |

    b. | 5 X 6   6 X 5 |

    c. | 8 ÷ 4   4 ÷ 8 |

    d. | 8 – 2   2 – 8 |

    e. | 1 ÷ 2   2 ÷ 1 |

    f. | 8 X 9   9 X 8 |

4. Is $4 divided among 2 people the same as $2 divided among 4 people? Explain why or why not. Use a complete sentence.

    _____

    _____

    _____

5. Based on the examples above, what conclusions can you make about the commutative property? Use complete sentences to explain your thinking.

    _____

    _____

    _____

4—David's Division Dilemma

[1]Ms. Kamen drew a "danger" flag on the board.

[2]David said, "I think Ms. Kamen is trying to wake us up."

[3]Ms. Kamen said, "You're right, David, I have four division problems I want you to solve."

[4]Ms. Kamen wrote on the board the four problems shown below.

[5]David looked at the problems and said, "Now, Ms. Kamen, I'm in the 8th grade so I know how to do these problems!"

[6]Ms. Kamen said, "Okay, David, that's great, go right ahead."

[7]For A and B David got an answer of 4. [8]He wrote 0 for the answers to C and D. [9]Ms. Kamen, being a good teacher, thanked David for trying but told him that two of his answers were incorrect. [10]She told David that his answer to problem A was correct and asked him to show a check. [11]David said, "I know 12 divided by 3 is 4 because 4 X 3 = 12, so it checks." [12]Ms. Kamen agreed with David and reminded the class that in any division problem, the quotient (answer to division) times the denominator (the divisor) always equals the numerator (the dividend). [13]Ms. Kamen warned David that one of the problems had an answer of "empty set," which means that there would not be an answer that would check. [14]Can you help David correct his two mistakes?

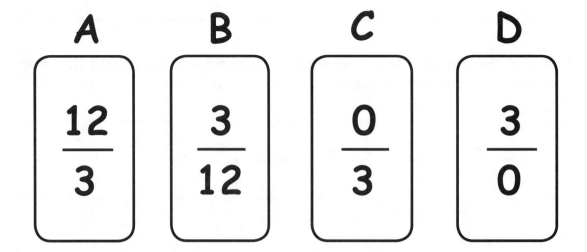

Questions

1. In problem A, the answer of 4 is also called the:

   a. divisor   b. dividend   c. denominator   d. quotient

   Give the number of the sentence that provides the best evidence for your answer.
   _____

2. David's answer to problem B was also 4. Use David's method of checking to show that his answer is NOT correct.

3. What is the answer to problem B? Use complete sentences to explain your thinking.

   a. 4   b. $\frac{1}{4}$ c. 3   d. $\frac{1}{3}$

   _____

   _____

4. The answer of 0 is correct for Problem C or D but not both. Show by using a check which problem has an answer of 0.

5. Think about the problem whose answer is "empty set." All of the following can help you find that answer EXCEPT the fact that

   a. 0 X 0 cannot be 3.
   b. a number can never be divided by zero because it won't check.
   c. if a problem does not check then the answer must be the empty set.
   d. dividing by zero gives an answer of zero.

6. The following day, Ms. Kamen put these problems on the board. Find each answer.

   a. $\frac{20}{4}$ _____   c. $\frac{0}{4}$ _____

   b. $\frac{4}{24}$ _____   d. $\frac{4}{0}$ _____

7. Another of Ms. Kamen's students asked her if it was possible to divide 0 by 0. Use complete sentences to explain how Ms. Kamen would answer.

   _____

   _____

5—The Amazing Mayans

[1]The Mayan civilization dates back to 400 A.D. [2]The Mayans were a large group of Central American Indians who lived mainly on the Yucatán Peninsula in Mexico.

[3]The Mayans were incredible mathematicians and astronomers. [4]They kept elaborate calendars and were able to keep track of the movements of the moon, the sun, and Venus. [5]They were also able to predict eclipses and the equinoxes with very accurate measurements.

[6]The Mayans had one of the most advanced number systems in the world. [7]They could represent very large numbers by using only three symbols. [8]Their number system was the first to include a symbol for 0 as a place value, while Europeans were still using the Roman numeral system.

[9]The Mayan number system is *vigesimal*, which means it uses base 20 instead of our decimal (base 10) number system. [10]The Mayans used only three symbols (see diagram A), and their numbers were arranged vertically (see diagram B). [11]Each step up was a power of 20, as illustrated below.

Diagram A

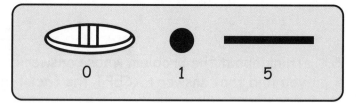

Diagram B

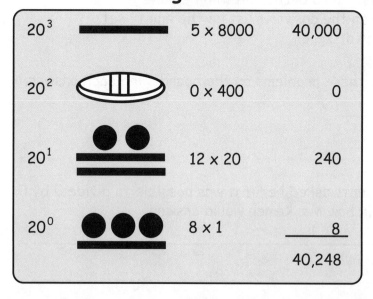

Source: Ascher, Robert and Marcia, <u>Code of the Quipu</u>.
Ann Arbor: The University of Michigan Press, 1981.

Questions

1. Write the number 500 using Mayan numerals.

2. Write the number 56,229 using Mayan numerals.

3. What is the next place value after 20^3 in the Mayan number system?

    a. 80

    b. 8,000

    c. 16,000

    d. 160,000

4. Subtract the smaller number from the larger number. Show your work.

    A.

    B.

5. Compare the Mayan number system with our number system. What is the same? What is different? Use complete sentences to explain your thinking.

    _____

    _____

    _____

    _____

6—The Planet Report

[1]Jennifer had to write a report on the planets. [2]She chose to research each planet's distance from the sun. [3]First, she made the chart below. [4]When she began to type her report, she realized that she was making too many mistakes typing zeros. [5]Her older sister Laura heard Jennifer complaining in front of the computer and asked her, "Jennifer, what planet do you live on? [6]Haven't you heard of scientific notation?"

[7]Laura explained to Jennifer that scientific notation was a short way of writing very long numbers. [8]Laura explained, "You have to follow some rules. [9]First, you put the decimal to the right of the first significant* digit and drop the unnecessary zeros. [10]Second, you write your decimal times a power of ten. [11]For example, 93,000,000 is written as 9.3×10^7." [12]Jennifer said, "Oh, I get it! [13]The exponent matches the number of zeros."

[14]Laura replied, "No, that's not true. [15]The exponent or power matches the power of ten you would multiply your decimal by to get back the number you started with. [16]Each time you move your decimal point to the right you are multiplying by a power of ten."

* In the number 306, the 0 is significant because it holds the important place value of the tens. However, in the number 5.0, the 0 is not significant because it doesn't change the value of 5.

Planet	Distance from Sun (in miles)
Mercury	36,000,000
Venus	67,000,000
Earth	93,000,000
Mars	140,000,000
Jupiter	480,000,000
Saturn	890,000,000
Uranus	1,800,000,000
Neptune	2,800,000,000
Pluto	3,700,000,000

Questions

1. To teach Jennifer about scientific notation, Laura used an example. Which planet's distance from the sun did she use? _____

2. Write the correct number next to each power of ten. Remember 10^3 means 10 X 10 X 10.

    a. 10^1 = _____   b. 10^2 = _____   c. 10^6 = _____   d. 10^9 = _____

3. Write 100,000,000,000 in words _____
    and by using a power of ten. _____

4. Show the results of multiplying 5.4 by each of these powers of ten.

    a. 5.4×10^1 = _____   c. 5.4×10^2 = _____

    b. 5.4×10^3 = _____   d. 5.4×10^4 = _____

    Explain how your answer is changing every time you increase the exponent. Use complete sentences to explain your thinking.

    _____

    _____

5. Neptune's distance from the sun in miles can be written as which of the following?

    a. 3.7 billion miles or 3.7×10^9 c. 2.8 million miles or 2.8×10^6

    b. 2.8 billion miles or 2.8×10^9 d. 1.8 billion miles or 1.8×10^9

6. How would you write the number 607,000,000 in scientific notation? Make sure to check your answer.

    a. 6.7×10^6 b. 6.7×10^7 c. 6.07×10^7 d. 6.07×10^8

7. When the base is 10, a positive exponent tells you to move the decimal to the right. Read sentence 16 again. What do you think happens every time you take a number and move its decimal point to the left? Use complete sentences to explain your thinking.

    _____

    _____

8. If 3.4×10^3 = 3,400, what is the answer to 3.4×10^{-3}? _____

7—The Percent Building

[1]In Sky-High City, there are no houses. [2]Every structure is a building with the same height and a different number of floors. [3]The ground floor is always reserved for parking. [4]Some tenants in some of the buildings live on the top floor. [5]The top floor is usually called the penthouse apartment.

[6]Mr. and Mrs. Lucas live on floor 3 of Building A. [7]Mrs. Kyong lives on floor 4 of Building B, which has a total of 10 floors. [8]Mr. Matsubara lives on floor 30 of Building C, which is known as The Percent Building because it has 100 floors. [9]Everyone wants to live in the Percent Building because the penthouse has a magnificent restaurant free for all the tenants who live there. [10]All of the tenants in the Percent Building are math detectives.

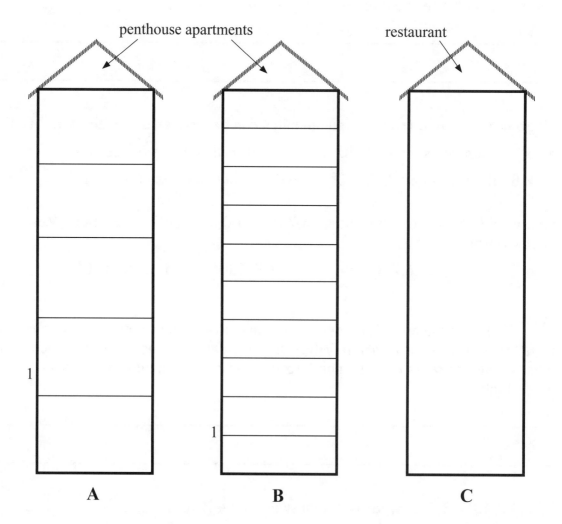

penthouse apartments

restaurant

A

B

C

Questions

1. What floor in Building B is at the same level as the floor that Mr. and Mrs. Lucas live on? _____ Show your work, using an equation with fractions.

2. Mrs. Kyong would like to move to the Percent Building, but she wants to live at the same level that she now lives on. What floor would she live on? _____ Show your work using fractions.

3. Mr. Baker lives on floor 80 of the Percent Building. His apartment door says 80%. What floor in Building A would be at the same level as his 80% apartment? _____ Show your work using fractions.

4. Which equation would best illustrate Mr. Matsubara's level if he were at the same level in a building of only 20 floors?

    a. $\frac{30}{100} = \frac{3}{10}$ c. $\frac{30}{100} = \frac{4}{20}$

    b. $\frac{30}{100} = \frac{6}{20}$ d. $\frac{30}{100} = \frac{15}{20}$

5. Who do you know for sure is a math detective?

    a. Mrs. Kyong

    b. Mrs. Lucas

    c. Mr. Matsubara

    d. Mr. Lucas

    Give the numbers of the two sentences that support your answer. _____, _____

II
OPERATIONS

8—The Roberts Family Reunion

[1]Ernest Roberts is organizing a reunion for his family in his hometown of Miami, Florida. [2]Ernest Roberts looked up the number of miles his only relatives would have to travel to come to the reunion.

[3]His sister, Louisa, lives the farthest from Miami. [4]She is hoping to drive 10 hours each day, and she can't wait to use her brand new jeep.

[5]Ernest's children, Cristina and Alexis, live in Washington, D.C. [6]Andy, Ernest's brother, lives 280 miles farther from Miami than Cristina and Alexis. [7]Andy is planning to take a plane to Miami.

[8]Cousin Esther and her children have rented a van to come to the reunion. [9]Esther estimates that if they travel an average of 70 mph, it will take them about 13 hours from their home to arrive in Miami.

[10]Ernest's aunts, Bertha and Emma, both live in Florida, but Aunt Emma does not drive, so Aunt Bertha (who lives farther north) will pick up Emma. [11]Then both will come together to the reunion. [12]Their cities are 140 miles apart. [13]The chart below lists the cities where all of Ernest's relatives live.

Distances to Miami, Florida (in miles)	
Los Angeles, CA	2720
Dallas, TX	1340
Washington, D.C.	1060
Nashville, TN	910
Orlando, FL	230
Jacksonville, FL	350

Source: http://www.travelnotes.org/NorthAmerica/distances.htm

Questions

1. Where does Esther live? Use complete sentences to explain your thinking.

   _____

   _____

2. Aunt Bertha drove 70 mph from her home to Aunt Emma's home without stopping. How long did this part of her trip take her? _____

   Give the number of the sentence that provides the best evidence for your answer.

   _____

3. It took Aunt Bertha four hours to get from Aunt Emma's house to the reunion. How many miles per hour was she averaging? Round to the nearest mile per hour. _____ Show your work.

4. If Andy's plane averages 380 mph, and he is taking a direct flight, how long is his flight? Round your answer to the nearest half-hour. Use complete sentences to explain your thinking.

   _____

   _____

5. If Louisa's jeep averages 60 mph, how many hours will she spend driving? Round your answer to the nearest hour. _____

   Give the number of the sentence that provides the best evidence for your answer.

   _____

6. What operation will you use to find out how many days it will take Louisa to drive to Miami?

   a. Multiply the number of driving hours by 10.
   b. Divide the number of driving hours by 10.
   c. Multiply the number of miles by 60.
   d. Divide the number of driving hours by 24.

   Give the number of the sentence that provides the best evidence for your answer.

   _____

9—Classroom Supplies

[1]It is the beginning of the school year, and Ms. Kamen needs to buy some supplies for her classroom. [2]The local stationery store gives Ms. Kamen a 10% discount because she is a teacher.

[3]Ms. Kamen finds out that glue sticks come in a box of 6. [4]Journals come in a pack of 8, and pens come in a box of 12.

[5]Ms. Kamen wants to buy the fewest packages to have exactly the same number of journals as pens.

[6]When Ms. Kamen goes to pay, the clerk forgets to take off the discount. [7]Ms. Kamen has to remind the clerk that she is allowed to pay $\frac{1}{10}$ less because she is a teacher.

Journals: pack	$7.50
Pens: box	$9.60
Glue sticks: box	$4.80

Questions

1. How many packages of journals and pens will Ms. Kamen buy? _____ (You can make a table to help you). Show your work.

   Give the number of the sentence that provides the best evidence for your answer. _____

2. How much does an individual journal cost? Round your answer to the nearest tenth. _____ Show your work.

3. What is the cost of one glue stick? _____ Show your work.

Give the number of the sentence that provides the best evidence for your answer. _____

4. If Ms. Kamen bought 3 packs of journals and 2 boxes of pens, how much would she pay before her discount? (Do not worry about tax.) _____ Show your work.

5. If Ms. Kamen bought 36 glue sticks, how much did she pay before her discount? (Do not worry about tax.) _____

6. Give the numbers of the two sentences that provide the best evidence as to how to find Ms. Kamen's discount. _____, _____

7. If Ms. Kamen spent $70.50 on classroom supplies, find the discount that she got and the total amount that she paid after the discount. (Do not include tax). Show your work.

Discount _____   Final Amount Paid _____

8. If Ms. Kamen spent $48.00 on pens (before tax and discount), how many pens did she buy? _____

10—Getting Ready for Track

[1]It was almost time for track season, and Tresela and Jewel wanted to get ready. [2]Mr. Bernstein, their coach, told the girls to keep track of how much they ran each day after school.

[3]Each girl recorded the number of miles she ran daily for one week. [4]Their charts are partly finished below. [5]Tresela ran a total of $21\frac{1}{4}$ miles that week. [6]One day, Jewel forgot to record how much she ran, but she knew it was twice as much as she ran on Wednesday.

[7]When Tresela saw how much Jewel ran, she told her, "Wow, that's a lot of feet you've covered!" [8]Jewel answered, "Yep, especially since a mile is 5,280 feet!"

Tresela	
Day	Miles
Monday	$1\frac{3}{4}$
Tuesday	$2\frac{1}{8}$
Wednesday	3
Thursday	4
Friday	$4\frac{1}{3}$
Saturday	
Sunday	0

Jewel	
Day	Miles
Monday	$2\frac{3}{4}$
Tuesday	4
Wednesday	$3\frac{3}{5}$
Thursday	5
Friday	
Saturday	$5\frac{1}{3}$
Sunday	$5\frac{3}{4}$

Questions

1. How many miles did Tresela run on Saturday? _____ Show your work.

   Give the number of the sentence that provides the best evidence for your answer. _____

2.   How many miles did Jewel run on Friday? _____ Show your work.

     Give the number of the sentence that provides the best evidence for your answer.
     _____

3.   On Tuesday, how many more miles did Jewel run than Tresela? _____ Show your
     work.

4.   What is the mean (average) number of miles that Tresela ran that week? _____
     Show your work.

5.   How many feet did Jewel run on Wednesday? _____ Show your work.

     Give the number of the sentence that provides the best evidence for your
     answer._____

6.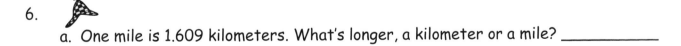

     a. One mile is 1.609 kilometers. What's longer, a kilometer or a mile? _____

     b. During that week, how many kilometers did Jewel run on the day she ran the
     most? (Round your answer to the nearest tenth of a kilometer.) _____ Show
     your work.

11—The School Election

[1]Student government elections were held at Boynton Middle School. [2]A student has to get a majority of the votes, or one more vote than half the number of total votes, to win. [3]Jenna reported the results in the school newspaper. [4]She stated that out of the total school population (all students were present), Maria got two-thirds of the votes for president. [5]Tom got two-ninths of the votes. [6]Sixty-four students, or one-ninth of the student population, abstained from voting (chose not to vote) for president.

[7]For vice-president, she reported that 499 students voted for Abdul, and the rest voted for Jim.

[8]For treasurer, she reported a tie between Ismael and Lori, so a new election had to take place the following week. [9]The following week on the day of the treasurer election, only 540 students made up the total school population because some were absent with the flu. [10]Ismael got 306 votes, and Lori got the rest.

[11]Lori complained in the student newspaper that she wanted another election. [12]She claimed that if all the students who were absent had voted for her, she would have won the election. [13]Ismael argued that even if all the absent students had voted for her, he would still have had the majority of the votes.

Questions

1. What is the population of Boynton Middle School? _____ Show your work.

    Give the number of the sentence that best supports your answer. _____

2. How many votes did Maria and Tom receive in the school election? _____ Show your work.

3. How many students voted for Jim? _____ Show your work.

4. What fraction of the students who were present the day of the treasurer election voted for Ismael? (Reduce your fraction to lowest terms.) _____

5. Is Ismael's argument correct when he says that even if all the people who were absent had voted for Lori, it would not make her the winner? Use complete sentences to explain your thinking.

_____

_____

_____

_____

_____

_____

12—Don't Spill the Black Beans!

[1]For his school's "dish to pass" event, Enrique wanted to share his mom's wonderful Cuban black bean recipe. [2]There are 24 students in Enrique's class, including Enrique. [3]His mom offered to help him make the black beans as long as he helped measure and cut the ingredients.

[4]When Enrique asked her to show him the recipe, she answered, "It's never been written down, but I've got it memorized." [5]Enrique became worried and said, "But my teacher wants us to turn in the recipe for a class recipe book." [6]His mom then said, "Well, get a pencil and paper and write down everything I do, but remember: this is how much I make for the six of us. [7]You'll have to figure out how to enlarge the recipe."

[8]Enrique wrote it all down and noted that 3 teaspoons (t) equals 1 tablespoon (T), 4 cups equals one quart, and 1 cup is 8 ounces (oz).

Ingredients

$\frac{7}{8}$ lb. dry black beans, $2\frac{1}{4}$ quarts water, 2 T olive oil (to soften beans)

Sofrito:

$\frac{1}{2}$ t oregano

$\frac{1}{4}$ t cumin

$2\frac{1}{2}$ t salt

2 t tomato sauce

$\frac{3}{8}$ cups olive oil

$\frac{3}{4}$ of a green pepper, chopped finely

1 onion chopped finely

3 garlic cloves, chopped finely

1 bay leaf

small piece of bacon (optional)

1 T sugar, 1 T vinegar

(author's authentic recipe)

Directions

1. Rinse the black beans in a colander. Watch for little pebbles. Don't spill any beans down the sink!

2. Let the beans soak overnight in the water in a large pot.

3. Next day, cook the beans in the water at medium high heat with the 2T olive oil. Cook them until they are soft (may take 2-3 hours).

4. When the beans are soft, make the sofrito.

5. In a large frying pan, heat the olive oil at low to medium heat and add all the sofrito ingredients, except for the sugar and vinegar, one at a time in the order given.

6. Take a big spoonful of the softened black beans and mash them into the sofrito to make a paste. Stir.

7. Take the sofrito paste and put it into the black beans. Stir well.

8. Add the vinegar and the sugar. You can add more salt and pepper to taste.

Questions

1. Did Enrique's mom have a copy of this recipe in her recipe file?_____

    Give the number of the sentence that provides the best evidence for your answer. _____

2. How many teaspoons are there in 2T of olive oil? _____

    Give the number of the sentence that provides the best evidence for your answer. _____

3. How many cups are there in $2\frac{1}{4}$ quarts of water? _____

4. What fraction of a tablespoon is $\frac{1}{2}$ teaspoon? _____ Show your work.

5. Enrique's mom has 8 cups of olive oil stored in a jar. How many sets of $\frac{3}{8}$ cups of olive oil can she get with that amount? _____ Show your work.

6. How many servings does the recipe that Enrique's mom dictated make? _____

    Give the number of the sentence that provides the best evidence for your answer. _____

7. Enrique needs to make so much food that his parents must help carry the beans. How many times should Enrique enlarge the recipe to feed his class, his teacher, and his parents? Use complete sentences to explain your thinking.

    _____

    _____

8. Here are some of the ingredients in the Cuban black bean recipe. Show the new measurements if Enrique needs to feed his class, his teacher, and his two parents. Show your work by each ingredient.

    a. _____lbs of black beans   d. _____c olive oil (for sofrito)

    b. _____quarts of water   e. _____onions

    c. _____T olive oil (to soften the beans)

13—The Taxi Investigation

[1]Mr. and Mrs. Baker and their two boys, ages 5 and 6, need to take a taxi from the airport to their hotel. [2]Their hotel is 12.5 miles away from the airport. [3]There are three main taxi companies that make trips from the airport, but their rates seem to be very different.

[4]Mr. and Mrs. Baker decide to eat dinner at the airport since the children are hungry, and during dinner Mr. Baker looks at the three charts below.

[5]Mr. Baker says to Mrs. Baker, "We should pick Orange Cab Co. since it will cost only $12.00 to get to the hotel." [6]She agrees.

BLUE CAB CO.
RATE FOR FOUR PEOPLE

First mile: $2.80

$.20 for each additional 1/8 mile or fraction thereof

Orange Cab Company

$6.00 PER PERSON

up to 10 miles. $.50 each mile per person after that

CHILDREN ARE FREE

(must be under 4 years old)

GREEN CAB CO.
RATE FOR FOUR PEOPLE

First mile: $3.20

$.15 for each additional 1/8 mile or fraction thereof

You pay two tolls: $1.20 each

1. How much would it cost the Bakers to take a Blue Cab to the hotel? _____
   Show your work.

2. How much would it cost the Bakers to take a Green Cab to the hotel? _____
   Show your work.

3. When Mr. and Mrs. Baker got to the hotel, they were really shocked at what they
   were charged. What was that amount? _____ Show your work.

4. What do you think is the most likely reason why Mr. Baker and Mrs. Baker made a
   mistake in choosing the Orange Cab Co.?

   a. They were told the wrong information.

   b. They did not know how to multiply correctly.

   c. They did not read the fine print.

   d. The chart was printed wrong.

5. If another cab company (the Purple Cab Co.) charged $4.00 for the first
   mile and $.25 for each additional $\frac{1}{8}$ of a mile, or fraction thereof, which of the
   following expressions represents the total amount charged? Let M stand for the
   total number of miles traveled.

   a. $4.00 + .25 X 8 X (M – 1)

   b. $4.00 + .25 X $\frac{1}{8}$ X M

   c. $4.00 + .25 X 8 X M

   d. $2.80 + 4 X $\frac{1}{8}$ + M

III
RATIO, PROPORTION, and PERCENT

14—Making Maple Syrup

[1]Maple syrup was an important part of the Native American diet. [2]Native Americans discovered that if they cooked the sap from maple trees, they could make a sweet delicious syrup. [3]The sap was cooked on an open fire. [4]Some of the same methods of making maple syrup are still being used today.

[5]Modern methods of collecting sap still include the basic techniques of tapping: make small holes, each 2 inches deep and $\frac{7}{16}$ inch in diameter, in the tree bark; then tubing is inserted to collect the sap. [6]This process doesn't hurt the trees. [7]Trees are tapped in late winter or early spring. [8]The sap runs when nights are cold and days are warm. [9]It must be boiled when it's fresh. [10]The color of the syrup depends on the season in which the sap was collected.

[11]It takes about 40 gallons of sap to make one gallon of maple syrup! [12]It also takes about five hours to boil down 5 gallons of syrup. [13]This is why pure maple syrup is so expensive.

1 pint (2 cups)	$7.50
1 quart (2 pints)	12.00
1 gallon (4 quarts)	32.00

Questions

1. Which of the following months is definitely not a good time to tap maple trees?

    a. March

    b. April

    c. early May

    d. August

    Give the numbers of the two sentences that provide the best evidence for your answer. _____

2. Is the width of the hole in the tree less than half an inch or more than half an inch? Why? Explain your thinking in complete sentences.

    _____

    _____

    Give the number of the sentence that provides the best evidence for your answer. _____ , _____

3. Over a three-week period, Dave collected 120 gallons of sap. About how many gallons of maple syrup will he be able to make? _____ Show your work.

Give the number of the sentence that provides the best evidence for your answer. _____

4. Six gallons of maple syrup is made from about how much maple sap? _____
Show your work.

Give the number of the sentence that provides the best evidence for your answer. _____

5. How many pints of maple syrup are there in six gallons of maple syrup? _____
Show your work.

6. How much would you save if you bought one gallon of maple syrup instead of the same amount in pints? _____ Show your work.

7. A cornbread recipe calls for $\frac{3}{4}$ cup of maple syrup. If you buy a pint ($7.50/pint) of maple syrup to make this recipe, how much are you spending for the $\frac{3}{4}$ cup of maple syrup? _____ Show your work.

15—Testing Time

[1]Ms. Kamen gave each student in her class a small piece of paper with the number of points they scored on a geometry test. [2]She said, "Many of you did very well, but a few of you need to study harder."

[3]Ms. Kamen wanted her students to figure out their percent score. [4]She reminded students that one way to find a percent is to make a fraction with their correct number of points as the numerator and 20, the total number of possible points on this quiz, as their denominator. [5]This fraction is then set equal to x over 100.

[6]The three best scores in the class were Carmen with 20 points or 100%, Rowan with 19 points, and Courtney with 18.5 points. [7]Ms. Kamen got upset with Rowan and Courtney because they began to brag out loud to the whole class about their points !

[8]Jackie whispered to Luis, "I didn't do so well on this test. [9]I got 1.5 points fewer than Rowan."

[10]Luis responded, "I don't know why you're feeling so bad. [11]I got 5 points fewer than Courtney earned."

[12]Tom, who was listening, whispered, "Well, at least one of you passed the test, and when my mom finds out my score, she'll ground me for life!"

[13]Ms. Kamen heard the whispering and added, "You should never compare yourself to anyone else. [14]Just do the very best job you can."

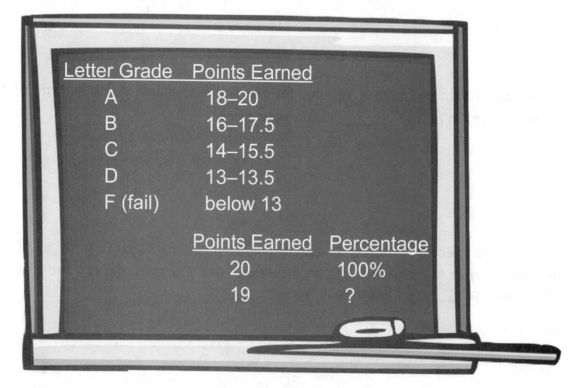

Letter Grade	Points Earned
A	18–20
B	16–17.5
C	14–15.5
D	13–13.5
F (fail)	below 13

Points Earned	Percentage
20	100%
19	?

1. What is the percent that Rowan scored on the geometry test? _____ Show your work.

    Give the number of the sentence that provides the best evidence as to how to find Rowan's percent on this test. _____

2. What percent did Courtney score on her geometry test? _____Show your work.

3. What letter grade did Jackie get on her geometry test? _____Show your work.

    Give the number of the sentence that provides the best evidence for your answer. _____

4. Which of the following CANNOT be Tom's score?

    a. 10 points
    b. 11 points
    c. 13.5 points
    d. 8 points

    Give the number of the sentence that provides the best evidence for your answer. _____

5. How many more points would Luis have needed to get a B on the geometry test? Use complete sentences to explain your thinking.

    _____

    _____

6. Which of the following is not a true proportion? (Remember, a proportion is two ratios or fractions that are equal.)

    a. $\dfrac{17}{20} = \dfrac{85}{100}$ c. $\dfrac{12.5}{20} = \dfrac{62.5}{100}$

    b. $\dfrac{8}{20} = \dfrac{40}{100}$ d. $\dfrac{16.5}{20} = \dfrac{84}{100}$

16—The 8th-Grade Dance

[1]The 8th-grade promotion dance is Friday night. [2]One hundred twelve 8th graders will be at the dance. [3]The ratio of boys to girls is five to nine. [4]Mr. Vann, the school principal, told the student council president, Sabina O'Connell, that she must ask enough teachers to chaperone. [5]Mr. Vann wants one adult to be present for every 14 students at the dance. [6]Sabina starts adding to the chart below to determine the number of chaperones she must ask.

[7]Sabina is also busy organizing a committee that will buy the pizza and put up decorations. [8]She finds out that a sheet pizza with 30 slices costs $16.99. [9]The student council only has $135.00 left in their account, and they must pay for the pizza.

[10]Luckily, the PTA is donating punch and cookies and will pay for all the decorations.

Boys	5											
Girls	9											
Total												
Chaperone												

Questions

1. If all the 8th graders are at the dance, how many of them are boys and how many of them are girls? You can finish the chart above to help you.

   Boys: _____   Girls: _____

   Give the numbers of the two sentences that provide the best evidence for your answer. _____, _____

2.   If Mr. Vann will be one of the chaperones, how many extra adults will Sabina need to ask to chaperone the dance? _____

Give the number of the sentence that provides the best evidence for your answer.

_____

3.   If each student and every chaperone will eat two slices of pizza, how many sheet pizzas should Sabina order? _____ Show your work.

4.   If there is no delivery charge and no tax, how much will the pizza cost? _____ Show your work.

Give the number of the sentence that provides the best evidence for your answer.

_____

5.   Does the student council have enough money to pay for the pizza? Use complete sentences to explain your thinking.

_____

_____

Give the number of the sentence that provides the best evidence for your answer.

_____

6 .   Which of these equations would help someone find how many boys and girls are at the dance without making a chart? Let n be the number of small groups, each one with 5 boys and 9 girls. (5n means 5 times n)

a. $5n + 9n = 112$
b. $14n - 5n = 112$
c. $5 + 9 = n$
d. $9n - 5n = 112$

Use complete sentences to explain your thinking.

_____

_____

17—Eddie's Cat Rescue Gone Wrong

[1]Eddie and George were out playing ball one summer morning when they heard a cat crying from very high up in a tree.

[2]"Maybe I can climb up and rescue the cat," said Eddie.

[3]"No way!" said George. "That tree has to be taller than 30 feet."

[4]They began to argue, as friends sometimes do. [5]"I'll run home and call the fire department, and I'll bring a measuring tape to prove to you that I'm right about the height of the tree," George added.

[6]George ran home, and when he returned he found Eddie up in the tree with his pants stuck on a limb. [7]George said, "Eddie, what are you doing?"

[8]"I'm stuck!" Eddie said.

[9]George replied, "Don't worry, the fire department is coming!" [10]Eddie did not look happy.

[11]Meanwhile, neighbors began to gather around. [12]One of them helped George measure his shadow and the shadow of the tree. [13]George was 5' 6" and his shadow was 22". [14]By using proportions, George was able to figure out the height of the tree.

[15]Soon Channel 3 showed up and was interested in knowing the height of the tree. [16]George said, "I never knew knowing math would make me so popular!" [17]Eddie was now red with embarrassment, and the cat had climbed even higher up in the tree. [18]Luckily, the fire department arrived promptly and rescued both of them.

[19]When Eddie came down, George said, "Glad you're safe and the cat is safe, but I was right. [20]The tree is higher than 30 feet!" [21]Eddie didn't say a word.

x

14'

Questions

1. How many inches tall is George? _____ Show your work.

   Give the number of the sentence that provides the best evidence for your answer. _____

2. How many inches is the shadow of the tree? _____ Show your work.

3. Which of the following is true? The tree's height is in proportion to
   a. the length of George's shadow in the same way that George's height is in proportion to the tree's height.
   b. the length of its shadow in the same way that the length of George's shadow is in proportion to George's height.
   c. the length of its shadow in the same way that George's height is in proportion to the length of his shadow.
   d. none of the above.

4. Which of the following is one correct way to set up a proportion to find the height of the tree?

   a. $\dfrac{x}{168} = \dfrac{66}{22}$ c. $\dfrac{x}{14} = \dfrac{5.5}{22}$

   b. $\dfrac{x}{14} = \dfrac{5.6}{22}$ d. $\dfrac{x}{5162} = \dfrac{14}{22}$

5. Find the height of the tree. Show what proportion you used.

6. Which of the following is the geometric principle that allows you to solve the problem above?
   a. similar triangles
   b. Pythagorean Theorem
   c. the measures of the angles in a triangle add to 180
   d. laws of trigonometry

18—The Furniture Store

[1]The Franklin Furniture Store was having an "End of the Year" sale. [2]Lorena and her mom headed to the store. [3]They wanted to buy a new sofa and a table. [4]On the way there, Lorena took a closer look at all the ads.

[5]She said, "Mom, I don't think 40% off $790 is $574."

[6]Her mom said, "It must be, because that is what the ad says."

[7]Lorena replied, "But Mom, you've always told me not to believe everything I read in the newspaper!"

[8]Lorena's mom said, "Are you sure you remember how to find the discount?"

[9]Lorena then said, "Of course—I can change 40% to a fraction, or I can change it to a decimal, and then multiply it by $790 to get the discount. [10]I know I'm right!"

ALL SOFAS 40% OFF!
ALL TABLES 25% OFF!

QUEEN SIZE SOFA USED TO BE $790
NOW $574!!

OAK TABLE REDUCED FROM $400

LEATHER SOFA REDUCED FROM $900

SLEEPER SOFA USED TO BE $850
NOW $510

Questions

1. What fraction is the same as 40%? Reduce to lowest terms. _____ Show your work.

2. How do you write 40% as a decimal? _____ Use complete sentences to explain your thinking.

_____

_____

3. Find the discount amount and the new price of the leather sofa. Show your work.

    Discount Amount _____   New Price _____

4. Show evidence for Lorena's claim that the ad for the queen-size sofa is wrong. Use complete sentences to explain your thinking.

    _____

    _____

5. If Lorena's mom buys the sleeper sofa and the oak table, find how much she would pay after both discounts. Include an 8% tax. Make sure you check to see if both are correct. Show your work.

    Total after both discounts: _____

    Tax at 8% for both items: _____

    Total with tax: _____

6. Explain why or draw a picture to show that 20% off an item is the same as paying 80% of the original cost of the item.

7. When Lorena's mom went to pay, she was told that if she found the same oak table or sleeper sofa at any other store for less money, she could come back to Franklin's and be paid 110% of the difference. This means that she would get

    a. the total amount that she paid plus 10% of the total.
    b. the extra amount that she paid plus 10% of that amount.
    c. any future purchases in the Franklin Furniture store for free.
    d. 10% of the extra amount that she paid in Franklin's store.

19—The Better Deal?

[1]Jacob wanted to buy a used car. [2]The car cost $2500, and Jacob had saved only $500. [3]His grandfather wanted to help him and said, "You can give me your $500 as a down payment, and then you can pay me the difference over a two-year period. [4]However, I'll have to charge you 5% simple interest over a two-year period."

[5]Jacob did not understand what that meant. [6]His grandfather explained that to find simple interest you multiply the principal ($2000) times the interest rate (5%) and times the number of years (two years). [7]Jacob thought that was paying too much interest, so he checked at the bank.

[8]His bank offered to lend him the $2500 as long as he paid 6% compounded yearly over a three-year period. [9]Jacob liked this better because he could keep the $500 cash, and it would give him more time to pay the loan back.

[10]When he told his grandfather he would borrow the money from the bank, his grandfather said, "Are you sure that's the better deal? [11]When interest is compounded, you pay interest on the interest." [12]Jacob's grandfather made the chart below to help Jacob understand how to find compound interest. [13]Then he added, "Jacob, next time you really want something, try to save more money!"

	Principal	Rate	Interest
Year 1	$2500	6%	$150
Year 2	$2650	6%	
Year 3		6%	
Amount owed after 3 years			

Questions

1. How much interest will Jacob have to pay his grandfather if he borrows money from him? _____ Show your work.

   Give the number of the sentence that best supports how to find simple interest. _____

2. At the end of two years, how much will Jacob owe his grandfather if he borrows money from him? _____ Show your work.

   Finish the chart on the previous page to help you with the questions below.

3. On the chart, the principal at the beginning of year 2 represents
   a. an additional amount Jacob had to borrow once again from the bank.
   b. the original amount borrowed plus the interest for the first year.
   c. the principal times 6%.
   d. none of the above.

4. What does Jacob owe the bank at the beginning of year 3? _____

5. At the end of 3 years, how much money does Jacob owe the bank? _____

6. How much more interest would Jacob have to pay the bank compared to the interest he would pay his grandfather? _____ Show your work.

7. Explain what Jacob's grandfather meant when he said, "When interest is compounded you pay interest on the interest." Use complete sentences to explain your thinking.

   _____

   _____

IV
GEOMETRY
and
INTRODUCTION TO
TRIGONOMETRY

20—The Three Triangles

[1]Three students in Ms. Kamen's class were asked to graph three triangles. [2]One student was asked to graph Triangle 1 and connect these ordered pairs (x,y) in order: A (7, -1), B (10, -1), C (2, 5), and back to A (7, -1).

[3]Another student was asked to graph Triangle 2 and connect the ordered pairs in order: D (-2, 1), E (-2, 7), F (-8, 1), and back to D (-2, 1).

[4]The third student was asked to graph Triangle 3: H (-11, -5), I (3, -5) and J (-4, -2) and then back to H (-11, -5).

[5]All three students graphed their triangles correctly. [6]Zoe's triangle was a right triangle. [7]Kahji's triangle was scalene. [8]Callie's and Zoe's triangles were both isosceles. [9]Use a ruler to draw their triangles.

[10]Remember that an isosceles triangle is a triangle with two congruent, or identical, sides. [11]A scalene triangle is a triangle with no sides congruent.

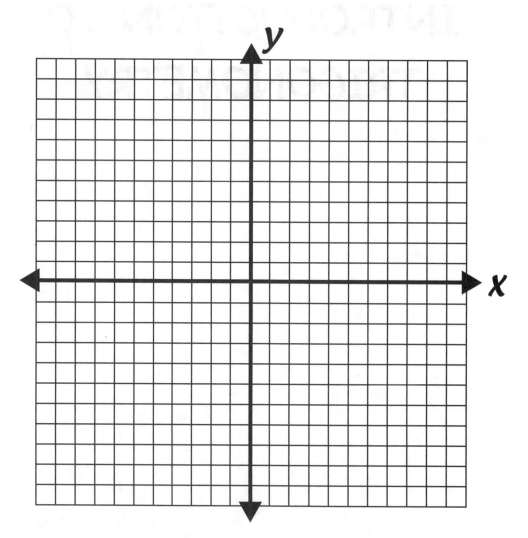

Questions

1. What is the number of the triangle that Kahji drew? _____ Use complete sentences to explain your thinking.

    _____

    _____

    Give the number of the sentence that provides the best evidence for your answer. _____

2. Which is the number of the triangle that Zoe drew? _____ Use complete sentences to explain your thinking.

    _____

    _____

    Give the numbers of the sentences that provide the best evidence for your answer. _____, _____

3. Which two sides of the right triangle are perpendicular? This symbol means perpendicular: $\perp$. $\overline{ED}$ means segment ED.

    a. $\overline{ED} \perp \overline{FD}$
    b. $\overline{CA} \perp \overline{AB}$
    c. $\overline{EF} \perp \overline{FD}$
    d. $\overline{HI} \perp \overline{JI}$

4. What is a more accurate name for Zoe's triangle?

    a. right scalene triangle
    b. obtuse triangle
    c. equilateral triangle
    d. isosceles right triangle

5. What is a more accurate name for Callie's triangle?

    a. equilateral triangle
    b. isosceles right triangle
    c. isosceles obtuse triangle
    d. scalene triangle

21—The Area Competition

[1]Tom and Toby were each asked to graph a triangle on the same grid. Tom's triangle is shown below. [2]He labeled his points T, O, and M. [3]Toby decided to label his triangle T, O, B, and his points T and O are the same as Tom's points T and O.

[4]Toby's ordered pairs were T (1, 1), O (7, 1), and B (10, 3). [5]Both students were told that the person whose triangle had the biggest area would win a prize. [6]They were both reminded that the area of a triangle is base times height divided by two.

[7]After Toby plotted his triangle, he said angrily, "There's no need to find the area of my triangle! [8]I can tell by looking at how skinny my triangle is that it must have less area than Tom's triangle!" [9]Toby refused to find the area.

[10]Tom said, "Great, I win!"

[11]Jenna, who was listening, said, "You guys! I don't think either one of you should win anything!"

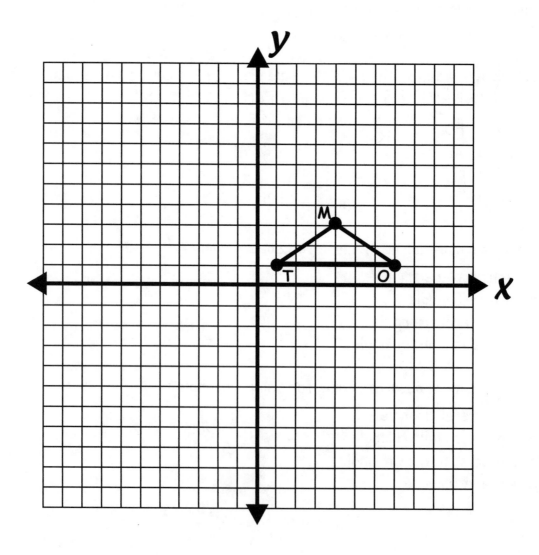

Questions

1.. What are the coordinates of point M in Tom's triangle?

   a. (3, 4)
   b. (4, 3)
   c. (4, 2)
   d. (2, 4)

2. Draw and label Toby's triangle on the same grid.

3. What is the base and the height of Tom's triangle?

   Base: _____ units   Height: _____ units

4. What is the base and the height of Toby's triangle?

   Base: _____ units   Height: _____ units

5. a. What is the area of Tom's triangle? _____ Show your work.

   b. What is the area of Toby's triangle? _____ Show your work.

   Give the number of the sentence that provides the best evidence for how to find the area of a triangle. _____

7. Was Jenna correct when she said that neither one should win anything? Use complete sentences to explain your thinking.

   _____

   _____

   _____

22—The Geometry Quilt

[1]Luis's mom is helping Maria and Luis make a quilt. [2]One of the quilt squares has a parallelogram (ABCD) on the right and two small quadrilaterals on the top and bottom (EFGH and JKLM), as shown below.

[3]Luis's mom wants to reflect parallelogram ABCD along the y-axis. [4]Maria asks, "Do you mean fold the vertical axis and draw the mirror image on the left side?"

[5]Luis's mom replies, "Yes, we will use the y-axis as the line of symmetry."

[6]Luis adds, "I think we should also reflect each of the small quadrilaterals along the y-axis so everything looks more symmetrical."

[7]Luis's mom adds, "Remember, some of our shapes may be quadrilaterals (four-sided shapes). [8]Some of these quadrilaterals may be parallelograms, and some may be trapezoids (quadrilaterals with <u>only</u> one pair of parallel sides).

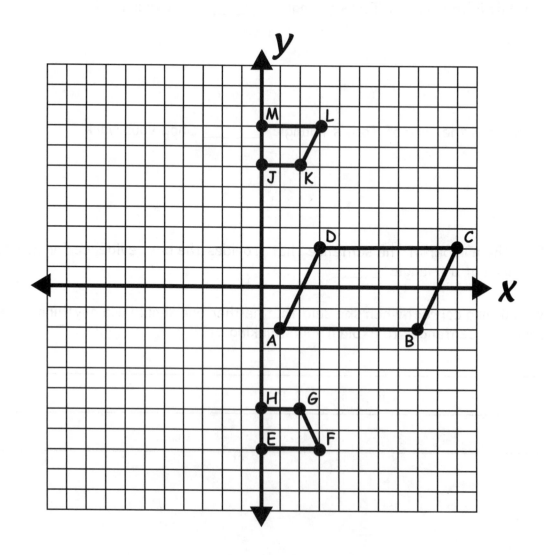

Questions

1. What makes ABCD a parallelogram?

    a. It has exactly four sides.
    b. It's a quadrilateral with 2 obtuse angles and 2 acute angles.
    c. It's a quadrilateral with opposite sides parallel.
    d. It is not a rectangle, so it must be a parallelogram.

2. List the ordered pairs that match points A, B, C, and D.

    A _____   B _____   C _____   D _____

3. What is a definition of a reflection? Use complete sentences to explain your thinking.

    _____

    _____

    Give the number of the two sentences that provide the best evidence for your answer. _____, _____

4, Draw the reflection of parallelogram ABCD along the y-axis on the same grid and label the corresponding points A1, B1, C1, and D1. List the new ordered pairs.

    A1 _____   B1 _____   C1 _____   D1 _____

5. Find the area of one of the parallelograms. Show your work.

6. Quadrilateral JKLM is a reflection of quadrilateral HGFE along which axis? _____

7. If you reflect quadrilateral EFGH along the y-axis, what new shape do you get? _____ Draw it on the same grid and label it using G1 and F1 as your two new points. Use complete sentences to define the new shape you got.

    _____

8. What is the area of the new shape you found in problem 7? _____ Show your work.

9. Reflect the top quadrilateral along the y-axis on the grid to see the final quilt square that Luis and Maria made. Label your two new points K1 and L1 (the reflection of K is K1 and the reflection of L is L1).

51

23—The Rectangle Resort

[1]The Baker family went on vacation last summer. [2]They stayed in a cabin. [3]The cabins were located six miles from the restaurant.

[4]The Bakers knew the distance from the tennis courts to the restaurant by looking at the map below. [5]They also knew that the restaurant, the cabins, the marina, and the tennis courts were at each corner of a rectangle because that is how the resort got its name.

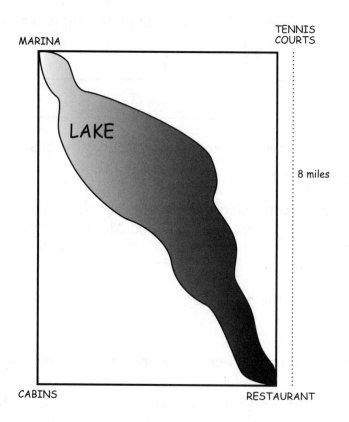

MARINA

TENNIS COURTS

LAKE

8 miles

CABINS

RESTAURANT

Questions

1. How far is it from the cabins to the marina? Use complete sentences to explain your thinking.

_____

_____

_____

2. How far is it from the marina to the tennis courts? _____

    Give the number of the sentence that provides the best evidence for your answer.
    _____

3. Find the area of the rectangle shown in the diagram. Show your work.

4. The Bakers wanted to take a boat from the marina to the restaurant. Find the
    length of the lake. (Use the Pythagorean Theorem $a^2 + b^2 = c^2$ where a and b are
    the sides of the rectangle and c is the diagonal, or hypotenuse.) Show your work.

5. What is the distance from the cabin to the tennis courts if you could travel across
    the diagonal of the rectangle? Use complete sentences to explain your thinking.

    _____

    _____

    _____

    _____

24—The Octopus Intersection

[1]In a certain quiet city there is only one busy intersection. [2]It's called the Octopus because so many roads intersect at the city park.

[3]Emily lives right on the corner of Buffalo Street and Albany Street. [4]Buffalo Street is perpendicular to Albany Street. [5]Her friend Rowan lives at the corner of Buffalo Street and Route 13. [6]Albany Street is parallel to Route 13.

[7]Dan lives on Route 96S while Terri lives on Route 96N. [8]Frank, Garrett, Mark, and Laura each live on the intersections marked by the first letter of his or her name on the map. [9]Mark lives two miles from Emily.

[10]The complete map of the Octopus intersection is shown below.

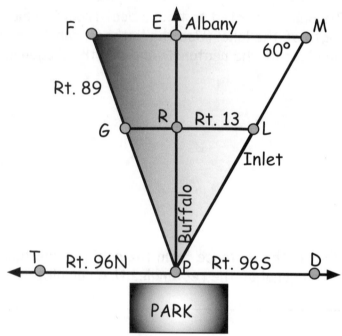

Questions

1. What is the measure of the angle that Albany Street makes with Buffalo Street? _____

    Give the number of the sentence that provides the best evidence for your answer.

    _____

2. Why is Buffalo Street perpendicular to Route 13? Use complete sentences to explain your thinking.

    _____

    _____

    Give the numbers of the sentences that provide the best evidence for your answer. _____, _____

3. Find the measure of the angle that Buffalo Street makes with Inlet Road at point P (<RPL). Use complete sentences to explain your thinking.

    _____

    _____

4. Find the measure of <RLP_____ (Hint: When two parallel lines are cut by a transversal their corresponding angles are congruent.) Use complete sentences to explain your thinking.

    _____

    _____

5. Two triangles are similar if their corresponding angles are congruent and their corresponding sides are in proportion. Name two triangles in the map that are similar and show why.

6. If <LPD is congruent to <GPT and the measure of <LPD is 65°, find the measure of <RPG. _____ Do not measure with a protractor. Use complete sentences to explain your thinking.

    _____

    _____

7. 🔺 If the distance from Mark's house along Inlet Rd. to the park (point P) is 4 miles, how many miles (round to the nearest tenth of a mile) are there from Emily's house along Buffalo St. to the park (point P)? _____Show your work.

    (Hint: Remember the Pythagorean Theorem, which states that in a right triangle $a^2 + b^2 = c^2$ where a and b are the legs of the right triangle and c is the hypotenuse.)

    Give the number of the sentence that provides the best evidence for your answer.

    _____

25—Soccer Abroad

[1]Micah and Steven are going to Romania with their soccer team. [2]Romania is a country in Eastern Europe. [3]Coach Kim gave the team the airline regulations for the size and weight of their luggage (shown below). [4]He warned, "You must follow these rules or you'll have to pay a lot of extra money. [5]You can bring one carry-on suitcase to take inside the plane and one larger suitcase to check in. [6]Don't bring anything else!"

[7]Steven said, "I don't get the 62 inches linear dimension rule."

[8]Coach said, "Add length plus width plus height and make sure your sum is no more than 62 inches."

[9]Micah asked, "Instead of adding, why don't they multiply the dimensions to get the volume and give people a list with volume restrictions?"

[10]Coach replied, "Micah, I have no idea—just follow the rules."

[11]Micah has a carry-on suitcase that measures 14" x 9" x 22" and weighs 21 lbs. after being packed. [12]The bigger suitcase that he wants to check in measures 7" X 24" X 32" and weighs 75 lbs. after being packed.

[13]Steven went shopping for a suitcase whose linear measures had a sum closest to 62", but whose dimensions multiplied to the biggest volume possible. [14]His smaller carry-on suitcase measured 21" X 13" X 9". [15]It weighed 10 lbs. when packed.

Airline Baggage Regulations

1 carry-on suitcase 22" X 14" X 9" (must weigh less than 20 lbs.)

Check-in items: 1 suitcase with linear dimensions, length + width + height no more than 62". (Items between 62" and 80" will be charged $80 extra.)

Check-in items must weigh no more than 70 lbs. (Items that weigh more than 70 lbs. up to 100 lbs. will be charged $110.00.) Items weighing more than 100 lbs. are not allowed.

1 in. = 2.54 cm.	1 lb. = .453 kg.
1 cm. = .39 in.	2.2 kg. = 1 lb.

Questions

1. Does Steven's carry-on suitcase meet baggage regulations? Use complete sentences to explain your thinking.

   _____

   _____

   Give the numbers of the two sentences that provide the best evidence for your answer. _____ , _____

2. Which of the following inequalities represents the required weight (W) in pounds of the carry-on suitcase?

   a. W < 20   b. W > 20   c. W ≤ 20   d. W < 70

3. Find the volume of Steven's carry-on suitcase. _____ Show your work.

   Give the number of the sentence that provides the best evidence on how to find the volume of the suitcase. _____

4. Will Micah have to pay extra for his bigger suitcase? If so, how much extra? Show your work. Use complete sentences to explain your thinking.

   _____

   _____

5. Below are several compound inequalities. Which one shows the range of the weight (W) that will result in a $110 charge for a check-in suitcase?

   a. W < 70 or W > 100   b. 70 < W < 100   c. 70 < W ≤ 100   d. 70 > W ≥ 100

6. Steven's dad had a suitcase he wanted Steven to check in. The linear dimensions had a sum of 157 centimeters and a weight of 30 kilograms (kg.) when packed. Would Steven have to pay extra? _____

7. Does Micah's carry-on suitcase meet the carry-on regulations? Use complete sentences to explain your thinking.

   _____

   _____

8. If Steven had found the suitcase he wanted (sentence 13), what dimensions would his suitcase have? _____ Draw a picture of his suitcase.

9. The coach asked the team why they thought the airlines uses the sum of the linear measures instead of a list of volume possibilities. Which answer is most logical?

    a. John: "Most people have tape measures instead of calculators, and they don't know how to multiply."

    b. Micah: "The airlines don't care about the volume of the suitcases."

    c. Tom: "The airlines use complicated rules to make work for their employees."

    d. Steven: "It's easier to add than to multiply, and the 62-inch limit helps keep the volume down."

26—The Tale of the Math Garden

[1]There once was a two-dimensional world where flat people lived.

[2]Some people had neatly arranged math gardens full of triangles, parallelograms, and circles of different sizes. [3]But the shapes mostly lay flat on the ground; they had only length and width.

Two-Dimensional Garden
(top view)

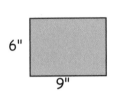

[4]One day, the flat people in this 2D world found a powerful powder. They sprinkled some on themselves and then on the ground. [5]Everything began to grow in height. [6]Luckily the people did not use too much of it, although some did.

[7]Below, the diagram shows how the rectangle, the triangle, and the circle from the 2D garden each grew in height. [8]Each 2D shape replicated itself, and identical layers grew on top of one another straight up to create 3D shapes no one had ever seen.

[9]Rectangular prisms grew from rectangles, and triangular prisms grew from triangles. [10]Circles became cylinders. [11]There were other beautiful shapes as well.

[12]The people, who were now no longer flat, began to ask themselves how to measure the space inside these 3D shapes. [13]One of them said, "For prisms and cylinders, the space inside the 3D shape must be the area of the original shape times the height it grew. [14]After all, the height is telling us how many layers we have."

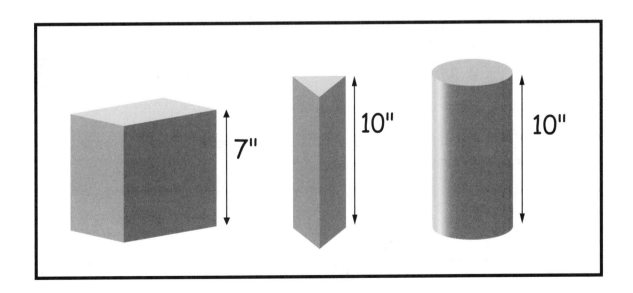

Questions

1. Find the perimeter and the area of the rectangle shown in the original math garden. Make sure to label your answers.

    Perimeter _____   Area _____

2. What is the formula used to find the area of a triangle? _____

    Find the area of the triangle in the original math garden. _____ Make sure to label your answer.

3. Find the circumference and the area of the circle in the math garden. Make sure to label your answer. (Remember $C = d\pi$ and $A = \pi r^2$ where d = diameter and r = radius. Use 3.14 for π.)

    Circumference _____   Area _____

4. What is another word for the amount of space inside a 3D shape?

    a. area   b. volume   c. perimeter   d. circumference

5. Which of the following is a prism?

    a. a cylinder   b. a box   c. a cone   d. a pyramid

    Give the number of the sentence that provides the best evidence for your answer. _____

6. If you put a cylinder on its side and cut the thinnest possible slice parallel to the base, what geometric shape do you get?

    a. an ellipse   b. a triangle   c. a circle   d. a square

7. Find the volume of each of the 3D shapes in the garden. Label your answer in cubic inches. Show your work.

    a. rectangular prism _____
    b. triangular prism   _____
    c. cylinder   _____

    Give the number of the sentence that provides the best evidence for your answers. _____

8.   One of the people in the math garden found the cylinder shown below with a volume of 1,570 cubic centimeters.

   a. What is the diameter of this cylinder? _____
      Rememember: the area of the circle (BASE) is πr². Use 3.14 for π.

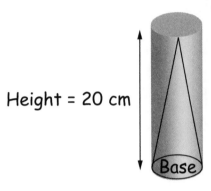

Height = 20 cm

Base

   b. If a cone with the same BASE and the same HEIGHT takes up $\frac{1}{3}$ of the volume, what is the formula for the volume of a cone?

      _____

27—Designing a Slide

[1]Students in Ms. Kamen's class are interested in designing a slide for the school's playground. [2]Ms. Kamen told her class that the ladder should be no more than 5 feet high. [3]Elijah drew the design below. [4]He decided to make the height of the ladder 4 feet.

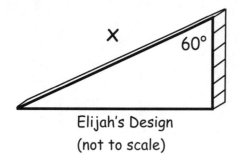

Elijah's Design
(not to scale)

[5]Another student, Latarsha, thought the angle of the slide was too steep. [6]She suggested keeping Elijah's height for the ladder, but changing to 70 degrees the angle that the ladder makes with the slide.

[7]Ms. Kamen reminded her students that the hypotenuse is the side opposite the right angle and that to find the length of the slide, they would need to use the trigonometry formulas below. [8]She pointed to the chart on the wall, which looked like this:

Sin <A =   opposite
            hypotenuse

Cos <A =   adjacent
            hypotenuse

Tan <A =   opposite
            adjacent

Trigonometry Table

Degrees	Sine	Cosine	Tangent
0	0.0000	1.0000	0.0000
5	0.0872	0.9962	0.0875
10	0.1736	0.9848	0.1763
15	0.2588	0.9659	0.2679
20	0.3420	0.9397	0.3640
25	0.4226	0.9063	0.4663
30	0.5000	0.8660	0.5774
35	0.5736	0.8192	0.7002
40	0.6428	0.7660	0.8391
45	0.7071	0.7071	1.0000
50	0.7660	0.6428	1.1918
55	0.8192	0.5736	1.4281
60	0.8660	0.5000	1.7321
65	0.9063	0.4226	2.1445
70	0.9397	0.3420	2.7475
75	0.9659	0.2588	3.7321
80	0.9848	0.1736	5.6713
85	0.9962	0.0872	11.4301
90	1.0000	0.0000	—

Note: Use the Trigonometry Table at the right to help you answer the questions.

Questions

1. In the diagram Elijah drew, the length (x) of the slide is the _____ of the right triangle.

    a. hypotenuse side

    b. adjacent side

    c. opposite side

    d. smallest side

2. In relationship to the 60° angle, the length of the ladder shows

    a. the adjacent side.

    b. the hypotenuse side.

    c. the opposite side.

    d. none of these.

3. Which of the following formulas should Elijah use to find the length of the ladder?

    a. $\text{Sin } 60° = \frac{4}{x}$

    b. $\text{Cos } 60° = \frac{x}{4}$

    c. $\text{Cos } 60° = \frac{4}{x}$

    d. $\text{Sin } 60° = \frac{x}{4}$

4. Which of the following is the design Latarsha wants to use for the slide?

    a.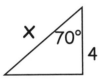

    c.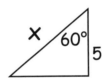

    b.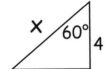

    d.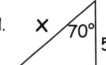

    Give the number of the sentence that provides the best evidence for your answer. _____

5. Find the length of the slide using Latarsha's design. _____ Show your work.

6. ✈ If the ladder is 4 feet, the hypotenuse is x, and the angle between them is 60°, which of the following is the same as $\text{Cos } 60° = \frac{4}{x}$?

    a. $\text{Sin } 30° = \frac{4}{x}$

    b. $\text{Sin } 30° = \frac{x}{4}$

    c. $\text{Tan } 60° = \frac{4}{x}$

    d. $\text{Cos } 30° = \frac{x}{4}$

V
PROBABILITY

28—The Potato Delight Store

[1]At the Potato Delight Store you can order a large baked potato for $4.00 including tax. [2]This includes one choice of toppings from each category. [3]Any extra toppings cost an additional 35 cents each.

[4]Louisa, Melinda, and Allen stopped at the Potato Delight Store after the movies. [5]Allen liked all the choices on the menu, but he didn't have a lot of money so he decided to pick only one choice from each category. [6]Louisa asked for American cheese, broccoli, mushrooms, and butter. [7]Melinda asked for a baked potato with all the toppings! [8]They each had a hot chocolate.

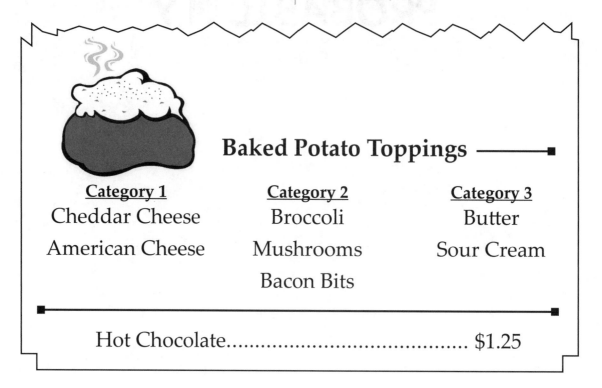

Baked Potato Toppings

Category 1	Category 2	Category 3
Cheddar Cheese	Broccoli	Butter
American Cheese	Mushrooms	Sour Cream
	Bacon Bits	

Hot Chocolate... $1.25

Questions

1. How many different types of baked potatoes could Allen choose? _____
    Show your work.

    Give the number of the sentence that provides the best evidence for your answer.
    _____

2. What is the probability that Allen will choose cheddar cheese, broccoli, and butter as one of his possible choices? _____

3. How much did Melinda's baked potato cost? _____ Show your work.

4. How much did Louisa pay for her baked potato and hot chocolate? _____ Show your work.

5. If Allen does not like broccoli, how many different types of baked potato could he make if he still has to choose one topping from each category? _____ Show your work.

6. How much did all three of them spend altogether, including the price for the hot chocolate? _____ Show your work.

29—The Display Dilemma

[1]Mrs. Wharton, the school librarian, just received a box of five new sports books for the library. [2]She wants to display them on the wall so students can see the front covers of the books.

[3]Mrs. Wharton can't decide whether she should put all five books up on the wall or just two at a time. [4]Three of the books are about soccer. [5]One book is about golf, and one is about ice hockey.

[6]One of the students reading at the library asks Mrs. Wharton if she can help. [7]Emily tells Mrs. Wharton that if she decides to put all five books on the wall and it matters what order they are in (see below*), then she has a lot of choices. [8]Emily explains, "You have five choices for the first slot on the wall, then four choices, three, etc.; then you multiply those choices. [9]This is called 5! or 5 factorial."

[10]She adds, "If you want to pick just two books at a time and the order matters, you have five choices for the first slot and four choices for the second slot. [11]Then you multiply those two numbers."

[12]Mrs. Wharton can't decide which books to show. [13]She says, "Thanks Emily, maybe I'll just pick two books without looking, and I won't worry about the order I put them in. [14]I just want more students to read as much as you do!"

* If the order matters, the arrangement S G I (Soccer, Golf, Ice hockey) is counted as being different from G S I.

Questions

1. How many ways are there to arrange 5 books on a shelf when the order doesn't matter? _____

   Give the number of the sentence that provides the best evidence for your answer. _____

2. Another way of writing 7 X 6 X 5 X 4 X 3 X 2 X 1 is to write 7!. Which of the following is 4! ?

   a. 4 X 3

   b. 44

   c. 24

   d. 64

3. If Mrs. Wharton picks two books out of the five and the display order matters, how many different arrangements can she make? _____

   Give the number of the sentence that provides the best evidence for your answer. _____

4. Mrs. Wharton decides to pick two books without looking and not worry about the order in which she places them on the wall. List the arrangements she can make. Use G for the golf book, I for the ice hockey book, S1 for the first soccer book, etc.

5. What is the probability that she will pick golf/ ice hockey (or ice hockey/ golf) in question 4? _____

30—The Custom License Plate

[1]Mrs. Rao wants to have a custom-made license plate for her brand new car. [2]She lives in a state where every license plate has three letters followed by three numbers. [3]Mrs. Rao would like to have a license plate that reads RAO 356: her last name, and the month and year of her birth (3/56) for March 1956.

[4]Mrs. Rao was told that she would have to pay extra to get exactly what she wants . [5]After paying for a new car, she does not want to pay the extra money, and she wonders what her odds are of getting RAO 356 by chance.

[6]Her neighbor Ted, who paid extra to get a license plate that reads TED 008 (Ted for his first name and 008 for the 8 children he has!), told Mrs. Rao that the odds of getting the license plate she wanted (without paying extra) were zero. [7]He said, "Remember, there are 26 letters in the alphabet and 10 digits, including 0, that have to be considered. [8]Repetition of the letters and digits is allowed. [9]Just getting RAO would be a chance of $\frac{1}{26}$ X $\frac{1}{26}$ X $\frac{1}{26}$." [10]Then he said, "You might have a better chance of winning the lottery."

Questions

1. How many different possibilities of license plates are there in the state where Mrs. Rao lives? _____ Show your work.

2. If her state has a population of 12,281,054, and each person had a car, how many possible extra license plates are there? _____

3.　Is Ted correct that Mrs. Rao's odds of getting the license plate she wants without paying are zero? _____
What is the probability of getting RAO 356 by chance? _____

4.　If repetition of the letters and digits was not allowed, how many different license plates would the state be able to issue? _____ Show your work.

5.　In sentence 10, the lottery that Ted was referring to is a lottery where you pick five numbers from 1 to 34, and repetition of the numbers is NOT allowed. Is Ted right that Mrs. Rao has a better chance of winning this lottery than in getting the license plate she wanted? Use complete sentences to support your thinking. Show your work.

_____

_____

_____

31—The Big Jolly Jelly Beans

[1]One Saturday in May, Amanda and Trevor remembered that there were still a few big Jolly jelly beans left in the candy jar. [2]They both liked the red and orange jelly beans best, so they began to argue about to how to share them.

[3]Their Uncle Mario decided that they each should reach into the jar without looking. [4]He told them that they could take only two turns each because it was almost time for dinner.

[5]The kids thought Uncle Mario's idea was a fair way to share the jelly beans until Amanda reached in (without looking) and got the orange jelly bean. [6]Trevor accused her of looking first, and they began to argue again.

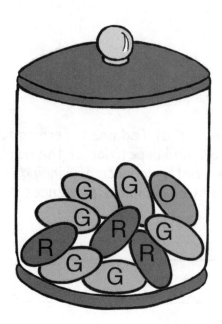

Questions:

1. What percent of the jelly beans are green? _____ red? _____orange? _____

2. What is the probability of reaching in (without looking) on the first try and getting the orange jelly bean? _____

3. If Amanda had eaten the orange jelly bean that she got on her first try, what would be the probability that Trevor would get another orange jelly bean from the jar on his first try?_____

4. If Amanda puts back the orange jelly bean because Trevor complained, what would Trevor's odds be of getting a red jelly bean on his first try?

    _____

5. If Amanda ate the orange jelly bean that she got on her first try, what is the probability that Trevor will get a red jelly bean on his first try? _____

6. Amanda got and ate the orange jelly bean. Then Trevor got the green jelly bean on his first try and and threw it away. What are the odds now that Amanda will get a red jelly bean? _____

7. After Amanda and Trevor had their first tries, all that is left in the jar are 5 green jelly beans and 3 red jelly beans. Are the odds of getting a red jelly bean now better or worse than getting an even number on a six-sided die (1, 2, 3, 4, 5, and 6 respectively on each side)? Use complete sentences to explain your thinking.

    _____

    _____

    _____

    _____

    _____

VI
STATISTICS

32—Winning the Shopping Spree

[1]Two electronics stores are advertising a chance to win a shopping spree to buy video games. [2]Store A claims that all its prizes will have a mean (average) value of $110. [3]Store B claims that all its prizes have the same mean value as Store A. [4]Liam knows both stores have great video games, and that's what he'll buy if he wins. [5]A raffle ticket will cost $10 at either store, and each store will have five money prizes to give away. [6]Liam can afford to enter only one raffle.

[7]Ben warns Liam that he should find out the amounts of the five prizes at each store before he buys his ticket.

[8]The charts below show the prizes each store will award.

Store A	
1st prize	$400
2nd prize	$ 80
3rd prize	$ 30
4th prize	$ 20
5th prize	$ 20

Store B	
1st prize	$160
2nd prize	$150
3rd prize	$120
4th prize	$ 90
5th prize	$ 30

Questions

1. Show that the mean of the total prizes awarded by each store is the same.

2. Why would knowing the mode (the most frequently used piece of data) be important for Liam to know? Use complete sentences to explain your thinking.

_____

_____

_____

3. Compare the range in the prizes awarded by each store. (The range is the difference between the largest and smallest number in each set of data.) Use complete sentences to explain your thinking.

    _____

    _____

    _____

    _____

4. Find the median for the prizes awarded by each store. (The median is the middle number when the data is organized from smallest to largest or from largest to smallest.) Show your work.

    Store A _____

    Store B _____

5. For each store, which data do you think was the most useful for Liam to know before making his decision?

    a. the mean

    b. the median and range

    c. the mode and mean

    d. the price of the raffle ticket

6. Liam entered Store B's raffle and won second prize! Taking into account what he spent to enter the raffle, how much money did he get? _____

    Give the number of the sentence that provides the best evidence for your answer.

    _____

33—The Battle of the Video Games

[1]Victor, Lupe, Latarsha, and Sarah are the only workers at their neighborhood video store. [2]During one Saturday, the store had a big sale.

[3]The worker who sold the most video games was promised a bonus of $1.49 for each video he or she sold.

[4]Latarsha sold twice as many videos as Victor. [5]Sarah sold one-seventh of the number Lupe sold. [6]Victor sold ten more videos than the number Sarah sold.

[7]The owner began to make a pictograph of the number of video games being sold. [8]He completed the line on the chart for Lupe, who sold 35 video games.

Latarsha	
Sarah	
Victor	
Lupe	▢ ▢ ▢ ▢

Questions

1   How many video games does this symbol represent?   ▢

   a. 1 video game

   b. 2 video games

   c. 5 video games

   d. 10 video games

   Give the number of the sentence that provides the best evidence for your answer.

   _____

2.   Complete the pictograph shown above.

3. How many video games did Sarah sell? _____

    Give the number of the sentence that provides the best evidence for your answer.
    _____

4. How many more video games did Latarsha sell than Victor? Use complete
    sentences to explain your thinking.

    _____

    _____

    _____

5. How many video games were sold in total? _____Show your work.

6. Who will get a bonus prize for selling the most video games?
    a. Latarsha
    b. Sarah
    c. Victor
    d. Lupe

7. How much money did the person who sold the most video games win? _____
    Show your work.

8. If y = the number of videos sold by Latarsha, which expression represents
    the number of videos Victor sold?
    a. $2 + y$
    b. $2y$
    c. $\frac{1}{2}y$
    d. $\frac{1}{7}y$

34—Great Books to Read

[1]Ms. Lutes, the school librarian, started to make a large poster with a bar graph of the five best-selling children's paperback books of all time. [2]She wanted to hang the graph (see below) at the school's new library.

[3]She started with *Charlotte's Web* by E.B. White. [4] *The Outsiders* by S.E. Hinton sold two hundred thousand fewer copies than *Charlotte's Web*.

[5]Judy Blume had the third bestseller, *Tales of a Fourth Grade Nothing*, with 7,100,000 copies sold. [6]*Love You Forever*, written by Robert Munsch, was the fourth bestseller. [7]The fifth bestseller was *Where the Red Fern Grows* by Wilson Rawls. [8]It sold two hundred thousand fewer copies than *Love You Forever*.

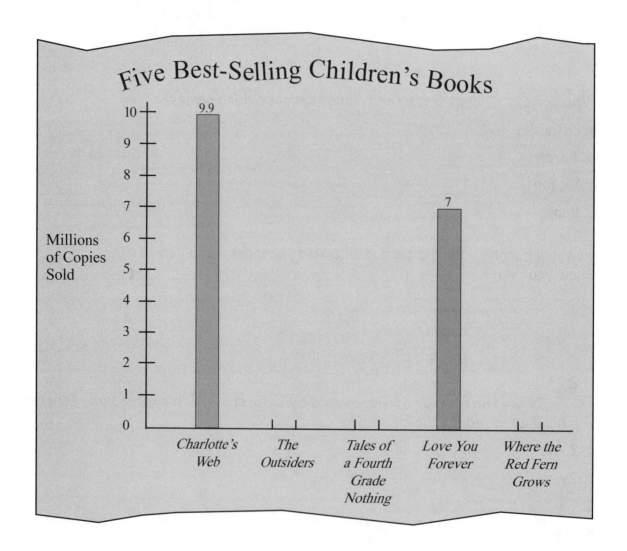

Source: *Time for Kids Almanac 2003 With Information Please*. Ed. Holly Hartman, New York, New York, 2002, p. 45.

Questions

1. 9.9 million copies is the same as

    a. 99 million copies

    b. 900,099 copies

    c. 9.9 copies

    d. 9,900,000 copies

2. How many copies of *The Outsiders* were sold? _____ Show your work.

    Give the number of the sentence that provides the best evidence for your answer.
    _____

3. Which of these is another way of writing the number of copies that *Tales of a Fourth Grade Nothing* sold?

    a. 7.1 million

    b. 7.1 thousand

    c. 7.1 copies

    d. 71,000,000

4. How many copies of *Where the Red Fern Grows* were sold? _____Show your work.

    Give the number of the sentence that provides the best evidence for your answer.
    _____

5. How many more copies of *Charlotte's Web* were sold when compared to *Where the Red Fern Grows*? _____Show your work.

6. How many copies in total where sold by all five bestsellers? _____ Show your work.

7. **Complete Ms. Lutes' bar graph.**

35—Dream-On Survey

[1]The editors of a school newspaper decided to do a survey about dreams. [2]They surveyed all 188 students in the school. [3]The editors found it interesting that of all the 100 girls in the school, all but two girls remember their dreams. [4]They also found it interesting that 44 boys dream only in black and white! [5]The results were partially filled out on the chart below. [6]The editors need the finished chart so they can publish it in the school newspaper.

	GIRLS	BOYS	TOTAL
Dream only in color	70		
Dream only in black & white	28		
Don't remember dreams		12	

TOTAL   _____   _____   _____

Questions

1. How many students in total do not remember their dreams?_____

    Give the number of the sentence that together with the chart helps you find the evidence for your answer. _____

2. How many students in total dream only in black and white? _____

3. What fraction of all the students in the school dream only in color? _____ Write your answer in the simplest form.

4. Compare the number of boys that don't remember their dreams to total boys. What is the ratio? _____ Write your answer in the simplest form. Show your work.

5. What percent of all the girls dream only in black and white? _____

6. Complete the dream survey chart.

7. One of the editors of the newspaper stated that 83% of all the students in the school dream. Is this report accurate? Use complete sentences to explain your thinking.

_____

_____

_____

_____

_____

36—Farming Our Town

[1]Last year, Friskie McDonald did a survey and printed a graph of the number of farm animals in her small town. [2]The neighbors thought the information was interesting, and they asked her to make a new graph this year.

[3]This year, Friskie found out that the Smith family, who raises pigs, had four times as many pigs as last year.

[4]The Velez family bought more land and added 40 cows to their dairy farm.

[5]Mrs. Burtless, who became the principal of the local school, informed Friskie that she had sold 10 cows, 13 sheep, and 29 goats to the Lee family, who had just moved into the town. [6]The Lee family had only the animals that Mrs. Burtless sold them.

[7]The Bakers told Friskie that their farm animal total had increased by 15%.

[8]This year, Friskie's going to start her own magazine and sell it for $.35. She'll name it "Farming Our Town." [9]Below is the double bar graph Friskie started to make to include in her magazine.

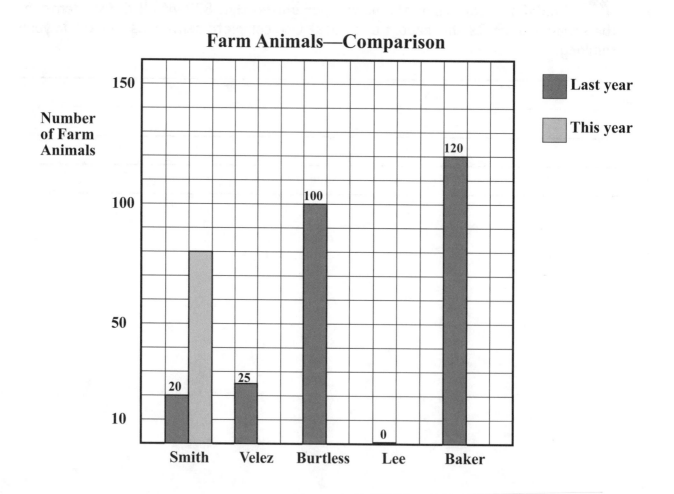

Farm Animals—Comparison

Questions

1. Complete the double bar graph.

2. What is the difference between the number of pigs that the Smith family had last year compared to this year? _____

   Give the number of the sentence that provides the best evidence for your answer. _____

3. What is the percent increase of farm animals in the Velez's family? _____

   Remember that to find the percent of change (increase or decrease), write a proportion: change amount/original amount = $\frac{x}{100}$ and solve for x.

   Give the number of the sentence that provides the best evidence for your answer. _____

4. What is the percent decrease for the Burtless family?
   Give the number of the sentence that provides the best evidence for your answer. _____

5. How many animals do the Bakers now have? _____ Show your work.

   Give the number of the sentence that provides the best evidence for your answer. _____

6. ✦ If a family has 100 animals, and they double the amount in one year, what is the percent of change? Use complete sentences to explain your thinking.

   _____

   _____

   _____

7. Friskie had to pay $24 to print her magazine. How many magazines will she have to sell before she begins to make a profit? _____ Show your work.

37—The Mean Rainfall

[1]A meteorologist in a city in Florida thought that it had rained a lot more than usual during the first eight months of this year. [2]So far, it had rained $1\frac{1}{8}$ inches in January, $2\frac{5}{8}$ inches in February, 2 inches in March, $3\frac{7}{8}$ inches in April, $2\frac{3}{4}$ inches in May, 4 inches in June, $8\frac{4}{5}$ inches in July, and $9\frac{1}{4}$ inches in August.

[3]The meteorologist did some investigating and decided to compare the rainfall the city had received so far with the mean (average) rainfall from previous years. [4]The mean rainfall is the average of all the months' totals taken for several years at the same location. [5]Rain is measured with a rain gauge.

[6]The meteorologist reported the results below. [7]He said on TV, "Things could be worse!"

Rainfall in Inches		
	Mean for Past Ten Years	Current Year
JANUARY	3	
FEBRUARY	2.8	
MARCH	4.2	
APRIL	3.9	
MAY	3.2	
JUNE	4.1	
JULY	9	
AUGUST	10.2	

Questions

1. What kind of graph would be best to use to compare the mean rainfall for the past ten years with the monthly rainfall the city received so far?

   a. bar graph

   b. line graph

   c. double line graph

   d. circle graph

2. Change the following data for these months from fractions to decimals. Show your work if needed.

   a. January $1\frac{1}{8}$ _____

   b. February $2\frac{5}{8}$ _____

   c. April $3\frac{7}{8}$ _____

   d. May $2\frac{3}{4}$ _____

   e. July $8\frac{4}{5}$ _____

   f. August $9\frac{1}{4}$ _____

3. How much less rain fell in April of this year compared to the mean rainfall for April over the past ten years? _____ Show work.

4. How much more is the total mean rainfall for the past ten years (January to August) compared to this year's total rainfall so far? _____ Show your work.

5. The mean rainfall in August was 10.2 inches. How do we know that it has probably rained more than 10.2 inches during that month in other years? Use complete sentences to explain your thinking.

   _____

   _____

   _____

   _____

6. On the grid provided on the next page, make a graph of the the rainfall for the first eight months of this year and the mean rainfall over the past ten years. Make sure to add a title, labels, and a key or legend for your graph.

7. Which month shows the greatest difference in rainfall from the ten-year average to this year? _____

38—Circle of Pizza

[1]On the day of its grand opening, Circle of Pizza, a new pizza place in town, asked the first fifty-four customers to pick their favorite topping.

[2]The owner wanted to make a circle graph of the results and enlarge it to cover one of the walls of the restaurant.

[3]Of the fifty-four people that were asked, nine said their favorite topping was mushrooms, and nine said green peppers. [4]Fifteen people said they preferred pepperoni, and eighteen said they preferred just cheese. [5]The rest said they preferred pineapple.

[6]Marisa, who works at Circle of Pizza, knew from her math class how to make a circle graph. [7]She told the owner that the graph had to show how each fraction of fifty-four related to the 360 degrees in a circle. [8]The next day, Marisa brought her protractor to work and began to show the owner how to draw the circle graph.

Questions

1. What fraction of the people surveyed like mushrooms? Write your answer in the simplest form. _____

   Give the number of the sentence that provides the best evidence for your answer. _____

2. Which of the following is true of the people surveyed on the first day?
   a. $\frac{1}{18}$ like pineapple.
   b. $\frac{1}{3}$ like green peppers.
   c. $\frac{1}{5}$ like green peppers.
   d. $\frac{1}{9}$ like just cheese.

3. Which of the following is true of the people surveyed on the first day?
   a. $66\frac{2}{3}$% of the people like pepperoni.
   b. $33\frac{1}{3}$% of the people like green peppers.
   c. $33\frac{1}{3}$% of the people like pineapple.
   d. $33\frac{1}{3}$% like just cheese.

4. How many degrees of the circle represent the number of people that like
    pepperoni? _____ Show your work.

    Give the number of the sentence that provides the best evidence for your answer.
    _____

5. If 216 people visit the new pizza place in one week, and the proportion of people
    who like pepperoni stays the same as for the first 54 people, how many people out
    of the 216 would say they prefer pepperoni? _____ Show your work.

6. Complete the circle graph below to show the results from the first 54 people who
    were surveyed. Use a protractor for accuracy. Your graph should contain labels and
    a title.

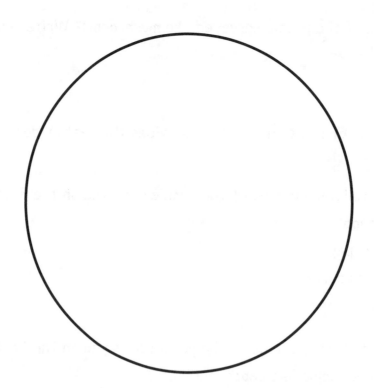

VII
ALGEBRAIC CONCEPTS

39—Expression Session

[1]Ms. Kamen had a contest to see which student could match the following mathematical expressions in the shortest amount of time. [2]She told her students, "Each of you has an envelope containing fourteen expressions. [3]Each expression matches another expression if their answers are equal. [4]You cannot start until I tell you to, and you must stop when I say stop."

[5]Ms. Kamen added, "Now, remember your properties. [6]The commutative property allows you to add or multiply in any order you wish. [7]The associative property allows you to change how you group your numbers as long as you are adding or multiplying."

[8]Eddie said, "Ms. Kamen, we know all this, let's start the game."

[9]Ms. Kamen said, "Well, Eddie, do you know the name of the property that allows you to say that $5(8 + 7)$ is the same as $40 + 35$?"

[10]Eddie answered, "The 5 is multiplying the sum of 8 plus 7, and that is the same as 5 times 8 plus 5 times 7, right? [11]I know it's the distributive property of multiplication over addition. [12]It also works for multiplication over subtraction. [13]You taught us well. [14]Can we start the game now?"

[15]Ms. Kamen smiled and said, "On your mark, get set, express yourself!"

[15]Below are the expressions Eddie received.

$30 \div 5 \cdot 6$	6^2	$\sqrt{36}$
$(3 + 9) + 8$	$5 \cdot 3^2$	$8 + (3 + 9)$
225	$3^2 - 3$	$27 - 24$
$3(9 - 8)$	$(5 \cdot 8) \cdot 9$	$5 \cdot (8 \cdot 9)$
	45	$(5 \cdot 3)^2$

Questions

1. Which expression matches with $\sqrt{36}$?

    a. 6^2

    b. $30 \div 5 \cdot 6$

    c. $27 - 24$

    d. $3^2 - 3$

2. When Ms. Kamen asked Eddie what property made the expressions (3 + 9) + 8 = 8 + (3 + 9), Eddie said "the associative property for addition." Is he correct? Use complete sentences to explain your thinking.

    _____

    _____

    _____

3. Explain why $5 \cdot 3^2$ and $(5 \cdot 3)^2$ are completely different expressions. Use complete sentences to explain your thinking.

    _____

    _____

    _____

4. Which two of Eddie's expressions represent the associative property?

    _____   _____

5. In the expression $30 \div 5 \cdot 6$, how do you know which operation to do first? Use complete sentences to explain your thinking.

    _____

    _____

    _____

6. Which set of Eddie's expressions represents the distributive property?

    _____

    Give the numbers of the two sentences that provide the best evidence for your answer. _____ _____

7. Show two ways of simplifying this expression: 4(25 - 3)

    _____   _____

8.   See how fast you can match Eddie's expressions.

1.	$30 \div 5 \cdot 6$	a.	$(5 \cdot 8) \cdot 9$
2.	$\sqrt{36}$	b.	$3^2 - 3$
3.	$(3 + 9) + 8$	c.	6^2
4.	$5 \cdot 3^2$	d.	$27 - 24$
5.	$3(9 - 8)$	e.	$(5 \cdot 3)^2$
6.	$5 \cdot (8 \cdot 9)$	f.	$8 + (3 + 9)$
7.	225	g.	45

40—The Bacteria Investigation

[1]Detectives were called to the science lab to investigate the amazing growth of some bacteria. [2]Dr. Bugnaru explained that given good growing conditions, bacteria could multiply very fast. [3]She said,

"Each cell forms two daughter cells. [4]Those two daughter cells, each with the same genetic make-up as the parent cell, will divide into four cells in only 20 minutes!" [5]Below is the chart she started to make.

Time (min.)	Number of Bacteria
10	2
20	4
30	
40	
50	
60	

Questions

1. How many bacteria cells are there after one half-hour? _____

    Give the numbers of the two sentences that provide the best evidence for your answer. _____, _____

2. Complete the chart above. How many bacteria cells are there after one hour?_____

3.   Which of the following expressions represents how the bacteria has grown after one hour?

   a. 6^{10}

   b. 2 X 60

   c. 2^6

   d. 6^2

Use complete sentences to explain your thinking.

_____

_____

_____

_____

_____

4.   If at one point, Dr. Bugnaru counted 8,192 bacteria cells, how much time had passed? _____ Show your work.

5.   Use the grid on the next page to graph the bacteria growth. You should get a curve. This type of graph is called a logarithmic graph.

The Bacteria Investigation

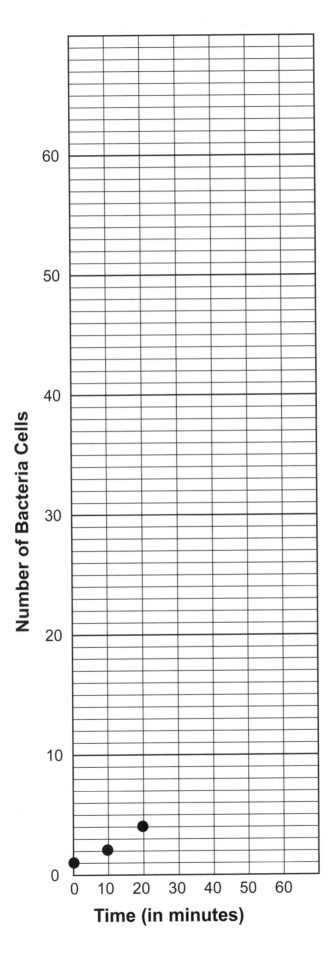

Number of Bacteria Cells

Time (in minutes)

41—Quane's Quarter Collection

[1]Quane is trying to organize her coin collection. [2]She's been saving quarters in a jar since she was little. [3]She hopes to put all her quarters in the bank when she has $100 worth of quarters. [4]On top of her jar, Quane has put a label with the chart shown below. [5]This helps her remember that "Q" is the number of coins in the box, and 25 is the value or worth of each quarter in cents.

[6]Quane started to record the quarters she now has. [7]She knew she would be getting more quarters for her birthday. [8]Then, for her birthday, Quane got 120 quarters from her parents and a bag of quarters from her brother Ben, who forgot to count them. [9]Later, Quane found out that adding what her parents and brother gave her to the amount she already had gave her a total of $56.50.

Before Quane's Birthday

Value of each quarter (cents)	Number of coins	Amount of money (cents)
25	Q	2125

Questions

1. How many quarters did Quane have before her birthday? _____ Show your work.

2. How many quarters did Quane get on her birthday? _____ Show your work.

Give the numbers of the two sentences that provide the best evidence for your answer. _____, _____

3. Finish this new label that Quane started to make for her jar. It represents the total amount of money she has after her birthday.

After Quane's Birthday

Value of each quarter (dollars)	Number of coins	Amount of money (dollars)
.25	_____	_____

4. How many more quarters does Quane need to reach her goal and deposit her money in the bank? Use complete sentences to explain your thinking.

_____

_____

_____

5. If a coin wrapper can fit 20 quarters, how many wrappers will Quane need to wrap $100 worth of quarters when she goes to the bank? _____ Show your work.

6. ⚑ Use the following variables to express the number of cents in "n" nickels _____ and "d" dimes _____.

7. Would you rather have 2,050 nickels or 410 quarters? _____ Use complete sentences to explain your thinking.

_____

_____

_____

42—Barrow, Alaska

[1]Barrow, Alaska is the northernmost city in the United States. [2]Only 1,300 miles from the North Pole, Barrow's temperatures range from -56° to 78° Fahrenheit (F). [3]The temperature in the summer averages about 40°F. [4]Wind chill temperatures play an important part in the lives of the people who live in Barrow. [5]When temperatures are cold, the wind can make it feel much colder. [6]The people in Barrow know how important it is to dress warmly and take precautions to prevent frostbite and hypothermia. [7]Below is a partial wind chill chart.

[8]Despite the arctic cold weather, Barrow is a beautiful, magical city. [9]On November 18th every year, the sun goes below the horizon and it doesn't come up again until January 24th. [10]Sunshine then begins to increase nine minutes each day until May 10th when the sun shines 24 hours every day!

Wind Chill Chart

Temperature — Degrees Fahrenheit

Wind Speed (mph)	20	15	10	5	0	-5	-10	-15	-20	-25	-30	-35
5	13	7	1	-5	-11	-16	-22	-28	-34	-40	-46	-52
10	9	3	-4	-10	-16	-22	-28	-35	-41	-47	-53	-59
15	6	0	-7	-13	-19	-26	-32	-39	-45	-51	-58	-64
20	4	-2	-9	-15	-22	-29	-35	-42	-48	-55	-61	-68
25	3	-4	-11	-17	-24	-31	-37	-44	-51	-58	-64	-71
30	1	-5	-12	-19	-26	-33	-39	-46	-53	-60	-67	-73
35	0	-7	-14	-21	-27	-34	-41	-48	-55	-62	-69	-76
40	-1	-8	-15	-22	-29	-36	-43	-50	-57	-64	-71	-78
45	-2	-9	-16	-23	-30	-37	-44	-51	-58	-65	-72	-79
50	-3	-10	-17	-24	-31	-38	-45	-52	-60	-67	-74	-81

Frostbite Times: 30 minutes   10 minutes   5 minutes

Source: http://www.weatherimages.org/data/windchill.html

Questions

1. What is the difference between the lowest temperature and the average highest temperature in Barrow, Alaska? _____

   Give the number of the sentence that provides the best evidence for your answer. _____

2. The temperatures for one week in Barrow during September are -11°F, -5°F, -3°F, 0°F, -4°F, 9°F, and 7°F. What is the mean (average) that week? _____
   Show your work.

3. One late afternoon in Barrow, the temperature is -30°F and the wind is blowing at 25 mph.

   a. What is the wind chill temperature when the wind speed is factored in? _____

   b. What is the frostbite time? _____

4. If the thermometer reads 5°F and the wind is blowing at 40 mph, how much colder is the wind chill temperature than the actual temperature?

5. If the wind chill factor temperature is -67°F and the temperature on the thermometer reads -30°F, how fast is the wind blowing? _____

6. ⚑ If sunshine begins to increase on January 24th, about how many days would it take for the sun to shine for 10 hours during one entire day? _____
   Show your work.

   Give the number of the sentence that provides the best evidence for your answer. _____

43—The Calendar Magician

[1]Eddie knew a calendar trick he liked to play on his friends. [2]He would show a month on the calendar and say, "Pick just four dates that touch each other, making a square. [3]Don't tell me which numbers you picked. [4]If you give me the sum of your four numbers, I'll tell you which numbers you picked."

[5]George looked at the month of March and picked the numbers in the square shown below. [6]He told Eddie only that the sum of his numbers was 28. [7]In a minute, Eddie told George what numbers he had picked.

[8]George thought Eddie just had a lucky guess, but when George said the sum of his numbers was 92, Eddie again was able to quickly determine George's four numbers.

[9]George eventually gave up and asked his math teacher how Eddie was able to guess his numbers so quickly. [10]When his math teacher saw the trick, he said, "It's algebra! [11]Eddie's not a calendar magician, but you, too, can do magic with algebra."

S	M	T	W	Th	F	S
	1	2	3	4	5	6
7	8	9	10	11	12	13
14	15	16	17	18	19	20
21	22	23	24	25	26	27
28	29	30	31			

Questions

1. If x is George's first number, how would you represent the number that is one unit greater than x?

    a. y

    b. $x + 1$

    c. $x + 2$

    d. $x - 1$

2. If x represents today's date, what expression represents the date that is a week from today?

    a. x + 7

    b. y + 7

    c. x – 7

    d. x + 6

3. If x represents today's date, what expression represents the date that is one week plus one day after today?

    a. x + 7

    b. x + 8

    c. z

    d. y + 1

4. Eddie was solving this equation in his head:
    x + (x + 1) + (x + 7) + (x + 8) = 28 or 4x + 16 = 28.
    What are the next two steps to solving the equation 4x + 16 = 28?

    a. Take the sum of 28, subtract 16 and multiply by 4.

    b. Take the sum of 28, add 16 and divide by 4.

    c. Take the sum of 28, subtract 16 and divide by 4.

    d. Take the sum of 28 subtract 16 and then subtract 4.

5. When George said the sum of his second square was 92, show how Eddie knew his numbers. Show your algebra equation and solve it.

6. When Eddie found out that George knew the secret, he came up with this problem for George. Think of a number, add 3 to it, multiply your sum by 6, subtract 10, and then subtract 8. Tell me your answer, and I'll know what number you were thinking of. George did all the work in his head and said his total was 30. Eddie said, "Ha, I know how you did it!" How did Eddie figure it out? Use complete sentences to explain your thinking.

    _____

    _____

    _____

    _____

44—Differing Degrees

[1]Alex's friend Marcos moved back to Spain after school got out. [2]Marcos called Alex on the phone and chatted a little bit in Spanish. [3]He told Alex the weather in Salamanca, Spain was 35 degrees Celsius! [4]Alex had no idea what 35 degrees Celsius meant. [5]Marcos laughed at Alex. [6]Marcos said, "In the United States, the Fahrenheit scale is used most often, but most of the world uses the Celsius scale."

[7]Alex found the Celsius/Fahrenheit chart on the right and kept it on the wall for the next time he talked to Marcos. [8]He also found two formulas he could use to convert from Celsius to Fahrenheit and vice versa. [9]Alex noticed that the way the Celsius scale increased by 5 and the Fahrenheit scale increased by 9 had something to do with how the formulas were derived.

Celsius	Fahrenheit
40	104
35	95
30	86
25	77
20	68
15	59
10	50
5	41
0	32
-5	23
-10	14
-15	5
-20	-4
-25	-13
-30	-22
-35	-31
-40	-40
-45	-49
-50	-58

To change from Fahrenheit to Celsius:

$$C = (F - 32) \cdot 5 \div 9$$

To change from Celsius to Fahrenheit:

$$F = C \cdot 9 \div 5 + 32$$

Questions

1. When comparing the formulas to the chart, Alex found that the Celsius scale

    a. changes by 5s while the Fahrenheit scale changes by 9s.

    b. changes by 9s and the Fahrenheit scale changes by 9s.

    c. is 32 degrees less than the Fahrenheit scale.

    d. is 32 degrees more than the Fahrenheit scale.

2. By using the chart, Alex found out that 35 degrees Celsius (35°C)is the same as what temperature in Fahrenheit? _____

3. When Marcos called back, he told Alex that his sister had a fever of 40°C. What temperature is that in Fahrenheit? _____

4. In the Fahrenheit scale, the freezing point of water is 32 degrees (or 0° Celsius). The boiling point of water is 212° F. What is the boiling point of water in Celsius? _____ Show the formula you would use and then show your work.

5. Around the December holidays, Marcos called Alex and told him the temperature was -20°F. What temperature is that in Celsius? _____ Round your answer to the nearest tenth of a degree. Write the formula you would use and then show your work.

6. At -40° the temperature is the same on both scales. Use an algebra formula to show why this is so. Let F = C and then solve for that variable.

© 2005 The Critical Thinking Co.™ • www.CriticalThinking.com • 800-458-4849

ANSWERS

I. NUMBER AND NUMERATION

1—The Summit Summer Camp

1. d. Sentence 5.

2. b. If Carlos is 14 and the twins are 4 years younger, then they are 10.

3. No. Martha and Luisa can sign up only for swimming lessons. They must be 12–13 to take the skating lessons.

4. c. Sentence 6.

5. Every 20 days. Soccer is offered every 4 days, skating every 5 days, and swimming every 2 days. Every 20 days he'll have the three classes at the same time [20 is the least common multiple of 4, 5 and 2]. 4 X 5 = 20, so 20 can be divided by 2.

6. 2 times. 40 ÷ 20 = 2. [There are 40 days of summer camp, and Luis has all 3 lessons every 20 days.]

7. Every 10 days. Rock climbing happens every 5 days, and swimming happens every 2 days. The least common multiple of 2 and 5 is 10.

2—The Prime Dart Game

1. a. Sentence 4.

2. A few possible answers:
   31 + 43 + 3 + 23 = 100 [in any order]
   37 + 43 + 17 + 3 = 100 [in any order]
   47 + 5 + 17 + 31 = 100 [in any order]
   Sentence 8.

3. c. [2 is the smallest prime number and the only even prime.]

4. 3 + 17 + 23 = 43
   Sentence 9.

5. The twin primes less than 100 are 3 and 5, 5 and 7, 11 and 13, 17 and 19, 29 and 31, 41 and 43, 59 and 61, and 71 and 73.

3—Let's Have Some Order!

1. Yes. Sentences 5,7,8.

2. a.

3. [Circle a, b, f; cross out c, d, e] These expressions hold true for the commutative property: 4 + 1 = 1 + 4, 5 X 6 = 6 X 5, 8 X 9 = 9 X 8. These do not hold true for the commutative property: 8 ÷ 4 ≠ 4 ÷ 8, 8 − 2 ≠ 2 − 8, and 1 ÷2 ≠ 2÷ 1.

4. No. $4 divided by 2 people is $2 per person whereas $2 divided by 4 people is $.50 per person.

5. The commutative property works for only addition and multiplication. It does not work for subtraction or division.

4—David's Division Dilemma

1. d. Sentence 12.

2. 4 times 12 [the denominator] is 48, not 3.

3. b. You can reduce $\frac{3}{12}$ to $\frac{1}{4}$. If you divide 3 by 12 [which is not the same as 12 divided by 3], you will get .25 which is $\frac{1}{4}$.

4. Problem C has a quotient of 0 because it checks: 0 X 3 = 0. The answer to Problem D is not 0 because 0 [the quotient] X 0 [the denominator] does not equal 3 [the numerator].

5. d.

6. a. 5; b. $\frac{1}{6}$; c. 0; d. Ø or empty set

7. It's not possible to divide 0 by 0. It could have many answers that check [for example, 0/0 = 5; 5 x 0 = 0]. The answer is the empty set. Accept an answer of infinity.

5—The Amazing Mayans

1.

1×20^2 or $1 \times 400 =$ 400
5×20^1 or $5 \times 20 =$ 100
0×20^0 or $0 \times 1 =$ 0
                                    500

Notice that 20 to the zero power or any number to the zero power [except zero to the zero power, which is undefined] is 1.

2.

7×20^3 or $7 \times 8000 =$ 56,000
0×20^2 or $0 \times 400 =$ 0
11×20^1 or $11 \times 20 =$ 220
9×20^0 or $9 \times 1 =$ 9
                                       56,229

3. d.
$20^4 = 20 \times 20 \times 20 \times 20 = 160,000$

4. 145
A is $(6 \times 400) + (8 \times 20) + (0 \times 1) =$ 2,560 and B is $(6 \times 400) + (0 \times 20) + (15 \times 1) = 2,415$

Subtracting B from A, $2,560 - 2,415 = 145$

5. Same: Both systems have a symbol for 0. Both systems are positional [there is a place value for each position where the digits or symbols are located]. Different: Our system is decimal [base 10] while the Mayan system is vigesimal [base 20]. Also, the Mayans used three symbols while our number system uses 10 symbols or digits.

6—The Planet Report

1. Earth.
2. a. 10
   b. 100
   c. 1,000,000
   d. 1,000,000,000
3. One hundred billion or 10^{11}
4. a. 54
   b. 5400
   c. 540
   d. 54,000.
   As the decimal point moves one place to the right, the number is ten times greater.
5. b.
6. d.
7. You are dividing the number by a power of 10, so the number gets smaller.
8. .0034. Move the decimal point to the left three spaces [divide by 1,000].

7—The Percent Building

1. Floor 6. Mr. And Mrs. Lucas live on floor 3 of Building A, which has 5 floors. $\frac{3}{5} = \frac{6}{10}$
2. Floor 40. $\frac{4}{10} = \frac{40}{100}$
3. Floor 4. $\frac{80}{100} = \frac{4}{5}$
4. b. $\frac{30}{100} = \frac{6}{20}$
5. c. Mr. Matsubara. Sentences 8 and 10.

II. OPERATIONS

8—The Roberts Family Reunion

1. Nashville. We know from Sentence 9 that if she travels 70 mph it will take her 13 hours.
   $13 \times 70 = 910$ miles [rate $\times$ time = distance]. Nashville is 910 miles from Miami, Fl.
2. 2 hours. 140 miles $\div 70 = 2$. Sentence 12.

3. 58 mph.
   Aunt Emma lives in Orlando [we know Aunt Bertha lives farther north].
   230 ÷ 4 = 57.5

4. $3\frac{1}{2}$ hours. We know Andy lives 280 miles farther from Miami than Alexis and Cristina, so Andy lives 1,340 [1,060 + 280] miles from Miami. He must be flying in from Dallas. 1,340 ÷ 380 mph = $3\frac{1}{2}$ hours.

5. 45 hours. 2720 ÷ 60 = 45.3 hours of driving time.
   Sentence 3.

6. b.
   Sentence 4.

9—Classroom Supplies

1. 3 packs of journals and 2 boxes of pens. Find the LCM [least common multiple] of 8 and 12 [8: 8, 16, 24, 32, ... and 12: 12, 24, 36, ...] The least common multiple is 24.
   Sentence 4.

2. $.94. $7.50 ÷ 8 = $.9375 which rounds to $.94.

3. $.80 [$4.80 ÷ 6 = $.80].
   Sentence 3.

4. $41.70. 3 journals @ $7.50 = $22.50 and 2 boxes of pens @ $9.60 = $19.20. $22.50 + $19.20 = $41.70.

5. $28.80. If she bought 36 glue sticks then she bought 6 boxes. 6 X $4.80 = $28.80.

6. Sentences 2, 7.

7. Discount: $7.05. Total after discount: $63.45.
   1/10 of $70.50 = $7.05 [or .10 X $70.50]. $70.50 - $7.05 = $63.45.

8. 60 pens. One solution: $48.00 ÷ $9.60 = 5 boxes of pens. Each box has a dozen, or 12, pens. 5 X 12 = 60 pens. Another solution: Each box has 12 pens, so each pen costs .80 [$9.60 ÷ 12]. $48.00 ÷ .80 = 60 pens.

10—Getting Ready for Track

1. $6\frac{1}{24}$ $21\frac{1}{4} - (1\frac{3}{4} + 2\frac{1}{8} + 3 + 4 + 4\frac{1}{4} + 0) = 21\frac{1}{4} - 15\frac{5}{24} = 6\frac{1}{24}$
   Sentence 5.

2. $7\frac{1}{5}$ $3\frac{3}{5}$ [Wed.'s time] X 2 = $7\frac{1}{5}$
   Sentence 6.

3. $1\frac{7}{8}$ mile. $4 - 2\frac{1}{8} = 1\frac{7}{8}$

4. $3\frac{1}{28}$. $21\frac{1}{4} ÷ 7 = \frac{85}{4} X \frac{1}{4} = \frac{85}{28} = 3\frac{1}{28}$

5. 19,008 feet. $3\frac{3}{5}$ X 5,280 $= \frac{18}{5}$ X 5,280 = 19,008.
   Sentence 8.

6. a. A mile is longer than a kilometer. It takes 1.609 kilometers to equal a length of 1 mile.
   b. 11.6 km. She ran the most on Friday. 2 X $3\frac{3}{5}$ = $7\frac{1}{5}$; $7\frac{1}{5}$ X 1.609 = 7.2 X 1.609 = 11.5848 or 11.6 km.

11—The School Election

1. 576 students. $\frac{1}{9}$ of the total population is 64, so 64 X 9 = 576.
   Sentence 6.

2. Maria: 384 votes ($\frac{2}{3}$ X 576 = 384)
   Tom: 128 votes ($\frac{2}{9}$ X 576 = 128)

3. 77 students. 576 – 499.

4. $\frac{17}{30}$. Reduce $\frac{306}{540} = \frac{17}{30}$ [See sentences 9 and 10.]

5. Yes, he's correct. Lori got 234 votes (540 – 306). If she had gotten all the votes from the 36 [576 which is total population – 540] people who were absent, then she would have 270 votes [234 + 36] which is one-half the total number of votes, but not a majority.

12—Don't Spill the Black Beans!

1. No.
   Sentence 4.

2. 6 teaspoons.
   Sentence 8.

3. 9 cups. $2\frac{1}{4}$ quarts = 8 cups + 1 cup because there are 4 cups in 1 quart.

4. $\frac{1}{6}$. $\frac{1}{2} \div 3 = \frac{1}{6}$ There are 3t in 1T and six $\frac{1}{2}$ tsp. in 1T, so $\frac{1}{2}$ t = $\frac{1}{6}$ T.

5. $21\frac{1}{3}$ sets.
   $8 \div \frac{3}{8} = 8 \times \frac{8}{3} = \frac{64}{3} = 21\frac{1}{3}$

6. 6.
   Sentence 6.

7. $4\frac{1}{2}$ times. He needs enough for 27 people [his class of 24 + 1 teacher + his 2 parents]. $\frac{27}{6} = 4\frac{3}{6} = 4\frac{1}{2}$

8. a. $3\frac{15}{16}$ or 3.9 or about 4 lbs. of black beans. $\frac{7}{8} \times 4\frac{1}{2} = \frac{7}{8} \times \frac{9}{2} = 3\frac{15}{16}$

   b. $10\frac{1}{8}$ q. water.
   $2\frac{1}{4} \times 4\frac{1}{2} = \frac{9}{4} \times \frac{9}{2} = 81/8 = 10\frac{1}{8}$

   c. 9T olive oil. $2 \times 4\frac{1}{2} = 9$

   d. $1\frac{11}{16}$ c olive oil.
   $\frac{3}{8} \times 4\frac{1}{2} = \frac{3}{8} \times \frac{9}{2} = \frac{27}{16} = 1\frac{11}{16}$

   e. $4\frac{1}{2}$ onions. $1 \times 4\frac{1}{2} = 4\frac{1}{2}$

13—The Taxi Investigation

1. $21.20. $2.80 [first mile] + (.20 X 8) [there are 8 one-eighth miles in each mile] X 11.5 [rest of the miles] = $2.80 + $18.40 = $21.20.

2. $19.40. $3.20 [first mile] + (.15 X 8) [there are 8 one-eighth miles in each mile] X 11.5 [rest of the miles] = $3.20 + $13.80 = $17.00. Adding $2.40 [cost of two tolls @ $1.20 each toll] = $19.40.

3. $29.00. 6 X 4 [the children are not under 4] + 2.5 miles [rest of the miles after 10 miles] X .50 X 4 people = $24 + $5.00 = $29.

4. c.

5. a.

III—RATIO, PROPORTION, AND PERCENT

14—Making Maple Syrup

1. d.
   Sentences 7, 8.

2. Less than $\frac{1}{2}$ inch. $\frac{8}{16} = \frac{1}{2}$, so $\frac{7}{16}$ is less than $\frac{1}{2}$.
   Sentence 5.

3. 3 gallons. $120 \div 40 = 3$ gallons
   Sentence 11.

4. 240 gallons. $6 \times 40 = 240$
   Sentence 11.

5. 48 pints. 1 gallon = 4 quarts = 8 pints, and $6 \times 8 = 48$.

6. $28.00. The cost of 1 gallon is $32.00. 1 gallon is 8 pints. $7.50 X 8 = $60.00. $60 - $32 = $28.

7. $2.81. 3/8 of $7.50 = $2.8125 or $2.81 (rounded to the nearest cent).

15—Testing Time

1. 95%. $\frac{19}{20} = \frac{x}{100}$; $190 = 20x$; $x = 95$
   There is another way to find percent: divide the numerator by the denominator and then move the decimal point to the right twice.
   Sentence 6.

2. 92.5% $\frac{18.5}{20} = \frac{x}{100}$; $20x = 1850$, so $x = 92.5$

3. B. $19 - 1.5 = 17.5$
   Sentence 8.

4. c. If he failed the test, he must have gotten a score below 13 points.
   Sentence 12.

5. 2.5 more points. $18.5 - 5 = 13.5$, so Luis got 13.5 points. To get a B he needed 16 points. $16 - 13.5 = 2.5$.

6. d.

16—The 8th-Grade Dance

1. Boys: 40. Girls: 72.
   Sentences 2 and 3.

2. 7. $112 ÷ 14 = 8$; $8 - 1 = 7$ more adults.
   Sentence 5.

3. 8. $112 + 8 = 120$ people X 2 slices per person = 240 slices. 240 slices ÷ 30 [number of slices in one sheet pizza] = 8 sheet pizzas.

4. $135.92. $16.99 X 8 = $135.92
   Sentence 8.

5. No, they have only $135, so they are short by 92 cents.
   Sentence 9.

6. a. 5n is the number of girls, and 9n is the number of boys in n groups. Adding 5n and 9n, you get 14n. So, $14n = 112$. If 14 times n equals 112, then $n = 8$.

17—Eddie's Cat Rescue Gone Wrong

1. 66". $5' = 60"$; $60" + 6" = 66"$
   Sentence 13.

2. 168". $14' X 12 = 168"$

3. c.

4. a.

5. 504" or 42'. $x/168 = 66/22$ Solving for x: $22x = 11,088$ and $x = 504$.

6. a.

18—The Furniture Store

1. $\frac{2}{5}$. $40\% = \frac{40}{540} = \frac{4}{10} = \frac{2}{5}$

2. .40   40% is the same as 40 hundredths, or .40

3. Discount: $360.
   New Price: $540. $900 X .40 = $360; $900 - $360 = $540.

4. The sofas are 40% off, so $790 X .40 = $316 [discount], and $790 - $316 = $474, not $574.

5. Total after both discounts: $810. Sleeper sofa: $850 X .40 = $340; $850 - $340 = $510. Oak Table: $400 X .25 = $100, $400 - $100 = 300. Add the new prices: $510 + $300 = $810. Tax at 8% for both items: $64.80.

.08 X $810 = $64.80.
Total with tax: $874.80.
$810 + $64.80 = $874.80.

6. When you take 20% off, an item now costs 80% of what it used to because $100\% - 20\% = 80\%$. A quicker way to find out the new price of an item that is being discounted 20% is to multiply the original cost by 80%.

7. b. The key word is "difference" at the end of the sentence. For example, if the table were sold for $5 less somewhere else, she would get $5 + .50 = $5.50 from Franklin's.

19—The Better Deal?

1. $200. $2,000 X .05 X 2 = $200.
   Sentence 6.

2. $2,200. $2,000 (borrowed) + $200.

3. b.

	Principal	Rate	Interest
Year 1	$2500	6%	$150
Year 2	$2650	6%	$159
Year 3	$2809	6%	$168.54
Amount owed after 3 years	$2977.54		

Year 1: $2,500 X .06 = $150. Year 2: $2,650 [adding $2,500 plus the $150 interest] X .06 = $159. Year 3: $2809 [$2650 + the $159 interest] X .06 = $168.54. Amount owed after Year 3: $2,977.54 [$2809 + $168.54].

4. $2809 [see chart]

5. $2977.54 [see chart]

6. $277.54 extra. $2,977.54 - $2,500 = $477.54 and $477.54 - $200 = $277.54.

7. In compound interest, the interest is added to the principal amount and then interest is added on the new amount, so you are also paying interest on the interest.

IV. GEOMETRY

20—The Three Triangles

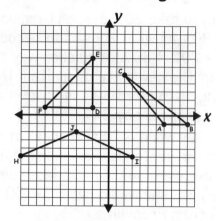

1. 1. Kajhi's triangle is #1 because his triangle is the only one that is scalene [no sides congruent].
Sentence 7.

2. 2. Zoe's triangle is #2 because she drew a right triangle [one having a right angle] and it's also isosceles [two sides congruent].
Sentences 6, 8.

3. a. [Segment ED is perpendicular to, or forms a 90° angle with, segment FD.]

4. d.

5. c. An isosceles obtuse triangle is one with two congruent, or identical, sides and an angle greater than 90°.

21—The Area Competition

1. b. From (0, 0) you go over 4 on the x-axis and then up 3 on the y-axis.

2.

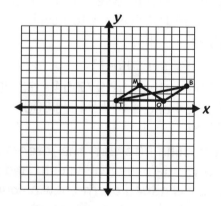

3. Tom: Base 6, Height 2

4. Toby: Base 6 , Height 2

5. a. 6 square units.
   b. 6 square units.
   Sentence 6.

6. Jenna was right. They both had triangles with the same area. Toby should have tried to find the area. Tom should not win since his triangle did not have a larger area. Accept answers that differ as long as they are mathematically correct.

22—The Geometry Quilt

1. c.

2. A (1, -2); B (8, -2); C (10, 2); D (3, 2)

3. A reflection is a mirror image along a line of symmetry.
Sentences 4, 5

4. A1 = (-1, -2); B1 = (-8, -2); C1 = (-10, 2); D1 = (-3, 2)

5. 28 square units. A= bh [base times height]. 7 X 4 = 28.

6. x axis.

7. trapezoid.
It's a shape that has two parallel sides.

8. 10 square units. Add the two bases [the bases are the sides that are parallel], multiply by the height, and divide by 2. Formula: $\frac{1}{2}$(b +B)h. The bottom base is 6; the top base is 4.
6 + 4 = 10; 10 X 2 [height] ÷ 2 = 10.
Notice that if you multiply by 2 and divide by 2 you get 1.

9.

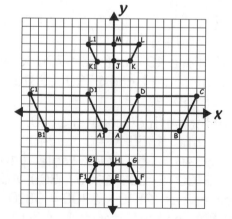

23—The Rectangle Resort

1. 8 miles. It has to be the same distance as from the tennis courts to the restaurant since in any rectangle the opposite sides are congruent.

2. 6 miles.
   Sentence 3. [same reasoning as above]

3. 48 sq. miles (6 X 8). The area of a rectangle is bh [base times height].

4. 10 miles. In any right triangle $a^2 + b^2 = c^2$ where a and b are the legs of the right triangle and c is the longer side or the hypotenuse. $6^2 + 8^2 = c^2$; $36 + 64 = c^2$; $100 = c^2$. Take the square root of both sides. $\sqrt{100} = 10$, so c = 10.

5. 10 miles. In any rectangle the diagonals are congruent.

24—The Octopus Intersection

1. 90°.
   Sentence 4.

2. We know Albany St. and Rt. 13 are parallel [sentence 6]. We know the measure of <MER = 90° [since Albany St. and Buffalo are perpendicular by sentence 4]. The measure of <LRP = 90° because when lines are parallel, corresponding angles are congruent [see note below]. Therefore, Buffalo St. is also perpendicular to Rt. 13. Two lines or segments that form right angles are perpendicular.
   Note: The converse is also true. When two lines are cut by a transversal, if the corresponding angles are congruent, then the lines are parallel.
   Sentences 4, 6.

3. 30°. In any triangle [look at <MEP], the measures of its three angles add to 180°. If the measure of <M = 60° and the measure of <MER = 90°, then the measure of <RPL or <EPM = 30°.

4. 60°. <RLP is an angle corresponding to <M. When lines are parallel [as with Rte. 13 and Albany street], corresponding angles are congruent

[<M = <RLP].

5. Triangle MEP is similar (~) to triangle LRP or triangle FEP ~ triangle GRP. Triangles are similar when their corresponding angles are congruent. [Note: This will also mean their corresponding sides are in proportion.]

6. 20°. Line TD is 180° [180° – 30° - 65° - 65° = 20°]. EP is not perpendicular to TD.

7. 3.5 miles. a = 2, b = ?, c = 4; $2^2 + b^2 = 4^2$; $4 + b^2 = 16$. Solving for b: $b^2 = 12$, and b = $\sqrt{12}$ or 3.5 miles.
   Sentence 9.

25—Soccer Abroad

1. Yes. Steven's carry-on was 21 x 13 x 9, which was less than the 22 x 14 x 9 limit. The weight of 10 lbs. was also less than the 20 lbs. listed in the sign. Sentences 14 and 15.

2. a.

3. 2,457 cubic inches [cu. in. or in³]. 21 X 13 X 9 [length X width X height] Sentence 14.

4. Yes. $190. The measurements are 7" + 24" +32" = 63". He'll have to pay $80 for going over the 62" limit. He'll also have to pay $110 extra because the weight is over 70 lbs. $110 + $80 = $190.

5. c.

6. No. [157 cm = 61.23", so he is under the 62" limit. 30 kg = 66.2 lbs., which is under the 70 lb. limit.]

7. No. The dimensions are the same as those required, but his weight is 1 pound over the limit allowed.

8. The biggest volume would be that of a suitcase shaped like a cube! 62 ÷ 3 = 20.6 [rounded to the nearest tenth]. These dimensions would work, for example: 20" X 21" X 20". Suitcases shaped like a cube are not popular.

9. d.

26—The Tale of the Math Garden

1. Perimeter: 30" [(2 X 6) + (2 X 9) = 12 + 18]
   Area: 54 sq." [6 X 9]

2. A = 1/2 bh [1/2 X base X height]
   12 sq. in. [6 X 4 ÷ 2 = 12]

3. Circumference = 18.84 in [6 X 3.14],
   Area = 28.26 sq. in. or in². [3² X 3.14 or 9 X 3.14].

4. b.

5. b.
   Sentence 9.

6. c.

7. a. Rectangular prism: V = 378 cu. in.
   54 [area of the entire BASE] X 7.

   b. Triangular prism: V= 120 cu. in.
   12 [area of the entire BASE] X 10.

   c. Cylinder: V = 282.60 cu. in.
   28.26 [area of the BASE] X 10.
   Sentence 14

8. a. diameter = 10 cm. V = πr²h. 1,570 ÷ 3.14 ÷ 20 = 25; so r² = 25. Take the square root of both sides, r = √25 or 5. If the radius is 5 cm. then the diameter is 10 cm.

   b. $\frac{1}{3}$ [area of base x height] $\frac{1}{3}$ hπr² [the base is a circle]

27—Designing a Slide

This lesson is an introduction to Right Triangle Trigonometry.

1. a. The hypotenuse is the longest side of a right triangle.

2. a.

3. c. Cos 60° = $\frac{4}{x}$.
   Cos 60° = $\frac{1}{2}$. If $\frac{1}{2}$ = $\frac{4}{x}$, then x = 8.

4. a.
   Sentence 6.

5. 11.7' Cos 70° = $\frac{4}{x}$. Cos 70° = .3420.

See trig table. If $\frac{.3420}{1}$ = $\frac{4}{x}$,then x = 11.7.

6. a. Sin 30° [30° is the other acute angle of the right triangle] is defined as the opposite side (4) divided by the hypotenuse (x). If Cos 60° = $\frac{x}{4}$ [adjacent/hypotenuse], then Sin 30° [looking at it from the other angle] is opposite/hypotenuse, which is Sin 30° = $\frac{4}{x}$ [choice a].

V. PROBABILITY

28—The Potato Delight Store

1. 12 different types. 2 X 3 X 2
   Sentence 5.

2. $\frac{1}{12}$. Cheddar cheese, broccoli, and butter is 1 out of 12 possible choices.

3. $5.40. $4.00 + $1.40 [4 extra toppings @ .35 each]

4. $5.60. $4.35 + $1.25. She ordered only 1 extra topping.

5. 8 possible types. 2 X 2 X 2.

6. $17.50. Allen: $4.00 + $1.25 = $5.25
   Louisa: $4.35 + $1.15 = $5.60
   Melinda: $5.40 + $1.25 = $6.65
   Adding their totals: $5.25 + $5.60 + $6.65 = $17.50

29—The Display Dilemma

1. 120 ways. 5! or 5 X 4 X 3 X 2 X 1 = 120.
   Sentence 8.

2. c.
   Sentence 9.

3. 20.   5 X 4 = 20
   Sentence 10.

4. GS1, GS2, GS3, GI, S1I, S2I, S3I, S1S2, S2S3, S1S3.

5. $\frac{1}{10}$

30—The License Plate

1. 17,576,000.
   26 X 26 X 26 X 10 X 10 X 10
2. 5,294,946. 17,576,000 – 12,281,054
3. No. 1/(17,576,000)
4. 11,232,000.
   26 X 25 X 24 X 10 X 9 X 8
5. No, Ted is wrong. Mrs. Rao has a better chance of getting the license plate. Lottery chances: $\frac{1}{33,390,720}$. Chance at getting license plate wanted: $\frac{1}{17,576,000}$

31—The Big Jolly Jelly Beans

1. Green: 60%. Red: 30%. Orange: 10%. Green's probability = $\frac{6}{10}$ = 60%. Red's probability: $\frac{3}{10}$ = 30%. Orange's probability = $\frac{1}{10}$ = 10%.
2. $\frac{1}{10}$ or 10%. There are 10 jelly beans in total and 1 of them is orange.
3. 0. If Amanda eats the only orange jelly bean in the jar, then the odds of Trevor getting another orange jelly bean are $\frac{0}{10}$ or 0.
4. $\frac{3}{10}$ or 30%. If Amanda puts the orange one back, then there are a total of 10 jelly beans (original amount in the jar), and there are 3 red ones, so the probability is $\frac{3}{10}$ or 30%.
5. $\frac{3}{9}$ or $\frac{1}{3}$ or $33\frac{1}{3}$%. Now there are only 9 jelly beans in the jar and 3 of them are red, so the probability is $\frac{3}{9}$ or $\frac{1}{3}$ or $33\frac{1}{3}$%.
6. $\frac{3}{8}$. There are now only 8 jelly beans left in the jar and 3 of them are red.
7. The odds of getting an even number on a 6-sided die is better than getting a red jelly bean. The probability of getting a red jelly bean is $\frac{3}{8}$ and the probability of getting an even number is $\frac{3}{6}$. $\frac{3}{8} < \frac{3}{6}$.

VI. STATISTICS

32—Winning the Shopping Spree

1. The mean of total prizes awarded by each store is $110. For Store A, add $400 + 80 + 30 + 20 + 20 and divide the sum ($550) by 5. For Store B, add $160 + 150 + 120 + 90 + 30 and divide the sum ($550) by 5.
2. Knowing the mode will help Liam realize that in Store A there are 2 out of 5 chances of getting the lowest prize of $20. In Store B, there is a 1 in 5 chance of getting the lowest prize of $30.
3. The range of prizes for Store A is $380. The range for Store B is $130.
4. The median of Store A is $30 and the median of Store B is $120.
5. b. Since the mean at each store was the same, it did not give Liam that much information.
6. $140. He won $150, and since he spent $10, his net gain was $140.
   Sentence 5.

33—Battle of the Video Games

1. d.
   Sentence 8.
2. Latarsha 30, Sarah 5, Victor 15, Lupe 35.

Latarsha			
Sarah	
Victor		
Lupe				

3. 5; 5
4. 15. 30 [number sold by Latarsha] – 15 [number sold by Victor].

5. 85. [30 + 5 + 15 + 35]

6. d.

7. $52.15. .35 X $1.49 = $52.15.

8. c. He sold $\frac{1}{2}$ of what Latarsha sold.

34—Great Books to Read

1. d. Multiply 9.9 X 1,000,000.

2. 9,700,000. Subtract: 9,900,000 – 200,000.
Sentence 4.

3. a.

4. 6,800,000. Subtract: 7,000,000 - 200,000.
Sentence 7.

5. 3,100,000. Subtract: 9,900,000 – 6,800,000.

6. 40.5 million copies. Add: 9.9 + 9.7 + 7.1 + 7 + 6.8

7.

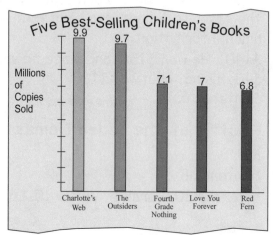

Five Best-Selling Children's Books

Charlotte's Web: 9.9 million, *The Outsiders* 9.7 million, *Tales of a Fourth Grade Nothing*: 7.1 million. *Love You Forever*: 7 million, *Where the Red Fern Grows*: 6.8 million.

35—Dream-On Survey!

1. 14.
Sentence 3.

2. 72.

3. $\frac{51}{94}$

4. $\frac{3}{22}$

5. 28%

6.

	Girls	Boys	Total
Dream only in color	70	32	102
Dream only in b & w	28	44	72
Don't remember	2	12	14
Total	100	88	188

7. It's not accurate. $\frac{174}{188}$ dream in color or black and white. That is 93% [rounded to the nearest percent] and not 83%.
$\frac{174}{188} = \frac{x}{100}$ and solve for x.

36—Farming Our Town

1.

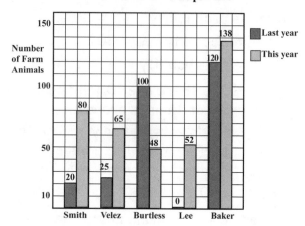

Farm Animals- Comparison

2. 60.
Sentence 3, also chart.

3. 160%. The change is 40. $\frac{40}{25} = \frac{x}{100}$
x = 160.
Sentence 4.

4. 52%. The change is 52. $\frac{52}{100}$ = 52%
Sentence 5.

5. 138. 120 + .15 X 120 = 138.
Sentence 7.

6. 100%. The change is 100. $\frac{100}{100}$ = 1 or 100%.

7. 69 copies. Divide 24 by .35. 68 copies only makes $23.80, whereas 69 copies makes $24.15. With algebra: Solve the inequality .35Y > $24 where Y is

the number of copies.

37—The Mean Rainfall

1. c.

2. a. $1\frac{1}{8}$ = 1.125; b. $2\frac{5}{8}$ = 2.625; c. $3\frac{7}{8}$ = 3.875; d. $2\frac{3}{4}$ = 2.75; e. $8\frac{4}{5}$ = 8.8; f. $9\frac{1}{4}$ = 9.25. To change a fraction to a decimal, divide the numerator by the denominator.

3. .025 Subtract: 3.9 - $3\frac{7}{8}$ = 3.900 - 3.875 = .025.

4. 5.975 Find the sum of the eight means over the past 10 years; subtract this year's total: 40.4 - 34.425.

5. The mean is the average. Although it's possible that for 10 years it has rained 10.2" every August, it's more likely that amounts higher and lower have fallen during the month of August.

6. March shows the biggest difference.

This Year's Rainfall Compared to the Mean Rainfall Last Ten Years

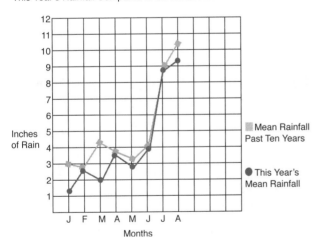

38—Circle of Pizza

1. $\frac{1}{6}$ $\frac{9}{54}$ = $\frac{1}{6}$
   Sentence 3.

2. a. $\frac{3}{54}$ = $\frac{1}{18}$ 9 [mushrooms] + 9 [green peppers] + 15 [pepperoni] + 18 [cheese] = 51, so the rest, which is 3, must be pineapple.

3. d. $\frac{18}{54}$ like just cheese, $\frac{18}{54}$ = $\frac{1}{3}$ or

$33\frac{1}{3}$%.

4. 100. $\frac{15}{54}$ like pepperoni, $\frac{15}{54}$ = $\frac{5}{18}$ = $\frac{100}{360}$.

Sentence 4.

5. 60 people. $\frac{15}{54}$ like pepperoni, $\frac{15}{54}$ = $\frac{5}{18}$ = $\frac{60}{216}$.

6.

Our First 54 Customers' Favorite Toppings

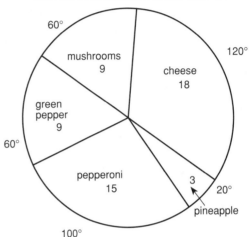

Mushrooms $\frac{9}{54}$ = $\frac{1}{6}$ = $\frac{60}{360}$ or 60 degrees. Same for green pepper.
Pepperoni: $\frac{15}{54}$ = $\frac{5}{18}$ = $\frac{100}{360}$ or 100 degrees.
Pineapple: $\frac{3}{54}$ = $\frac{1}{18}$ = $\frac{20}{360}$ or 20 degrees.
Cheese: $\frac{18}{54}$ = $\frac{1}{3}$ = $\frac{120}{360}$ or 120 degrees.

VII—ALGEBRAIC CONCEPTS

39—Expression Session

1. d. $3^2 - 3 = (3 \times 3) - 3 = 9 - 3 = 6$

2. No, it's the commutative property for addition. The number 8 is moving from the end to the beginning of the expression. The order has changed.

3. $5 \cdot 3^2 = 5 \cdot 9 = 45$; $(5 \cdot 3)^2 = 15^2 = 225$. Using the order of operations, in the first expression the exponent must be done first. In the second expression, the operation inside the parentheses

must be done first.

4. (5 · 8) · 9 = 5 · (8 · 9). The grouping has changed, but the order has stayed the same.

5. Division is done first. The order of operations must be followed in this order: Do parentheses, exponents, then multiplication or division [either one of these as you read the problem from left to right], then addition or subtraction [either one of these two as you read the problem from left to right].

6. 3(9 – 8) = 27 – 24
Sentences 9, 11

7. 4(25 – 3) can be done two ways. You can do the parentheses first and get 4 · 22 = 88, or you can use the distributive property. 4 · 25 – 4 · 3 = 100 – 12 = 88.

8. 1c, 2b, 3f, 4g, 5d, 6a, 7e

40—The Bacteria Investigation

1. 8.
Sentences 3, 4.

2. 64.

Time (min.)	Number of bacteria
10	2
20	4
30	8
40	16
50	32
60	64

Every 10 minutes the number of cells doubles.

3.c. 2^6 or 2 X 2 X 2 X 2 X 2 X 2 = 64. Every 10 minutes, the amount of bacteria is two times greater than it was the previous time. First there were 2, then 4,... until 64.

4. 130 minutes or 2 hours and 10 minutes. Time, #Bacteria: (10, 2), (20, 4); (30, 8); (40, 16); (50, 32); (60, 64);

(70, 128); (80, 256); (90, 512); (100, 1,024); (110, 2,048); (120, 4,096); (130, 8,192).

5.

The Bacteria Investigation

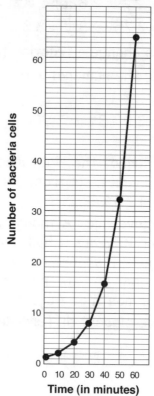

41—Quane's Quarter Collection

1. 85 quarters. $21.25 ÷ $.25.

2. 141 quarters. $56.50 [her new total] - $21.25 [what she had before her birthday] = $35.25. $35.25 ÷ $.25 = 141 quarters.
Sentences 8 and 9.

3. Number of coins: 226. Amount of money [in dollars]: $56.50. Divide the $56.50 given in sentence 9 by .25 to get 226 coins OR 85 + 141 = 226

4. She needs 174 more quarters. She has $56.50 or 226 quarters. She wants to have $100 (or 400 quarters) to put in the bank.
400 – 226 = 174.

5. She will need 20 wrappers. 400 quarters ÷ 20 per wrapper = 20 wrappers.

6. "n" nickels: 5n; "d" dimes: 10d.

7. They are both the same ($102.50). However, it may be easier to wrap 410 quarters than 2,050 nickels!

42—Barrow, Alaska

1. 1340. From -56 to 78 is 134 degrees. Sentence 2.
2. -1° Add: -11 + -5 + -3 + 0 + -4 + 9 + 7 = -7. Divide -7 ÷ 7 = -1.
3. a. -64° b. 5 minutes
4. -27 or 27 degrees colder.
5. 30 mph.
6. About 67 days. The sun increases 9 minutes per day. Ten hours is 600 minutes (10 X 60). Divide 600 ÷ 9 = 66.666.
   Sentence 9.

43—The Calendar Magician

1. b.
2. a.
3. b.
4. c. Use the inverse operations to help you solve the equation. The inverse operation of addition is subtraction, and the inverse operation of multiplication is division. Remember to always undo addition and subtraction first.
5. 4x + 16 = 92.   4x = 92 - 16.   4x = 76. x = 76 ÷ 4. x = 19. Since the first date is 19, the numbers in the square are 19, 20, 26 and 27.
6. If x is George's number, this is what he does in his head: (x + 3) • 6 – 10 – 8. Distribute the 6 and you get: 6x + 18

– 10 – 8, which is 6x. George said his answer was 30, so Eddie knew 30 was 6 times his original number. George's original number was 5.

44—Differing Degrees

1. a.
2. 95°F
3. 104°F
4. 100°C. Use this formula: C = (F – 32) • 5 ÷ 9. Substitute 212 for F, C = (212 – 32) • 5 ÷ 9 = 180 • 5 ÷ 9 = 100.
5. -28.9° C. Use this formula: C = (F – 32) • 5 ÷ 9. Substitute -20 for F,   C = (-20 – 32) • 5 ÷ 9 = -52 • 5 ÷ 9 = -260 ÷ 9 = -28.9 (rounded to the nearest tenth of a degree).
6. You can substitute -40 in each formula to confirm that you get -40 for both Centigrade and Fahrenheit. Using algebra: Use the Fahrenheit formula and let C = F. Now, F = F • 9 ÷ 5 + 32. You can write it as F = $\frac{9}{5}$F + 32. Subtracting $\frac{9}{5}$F from both sides, you get -$\frac{4}{5}$F = 32. This gives you -4F = 160, and F = -40. Then use the Centigrade formula: C = (F – 32) x 5 ÷ 9. If F = -40, then -72 • 5 ÷ 9 = -4, so C is also -40.